T0131799

POLITICS, FAITH, *Love*

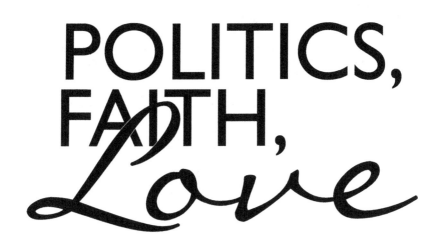

A Judge's Notes on Things That Matter

JUDGE BILL SWANN

BALBOA.
PRESS

A DIVISION OF HAY HOUSE

Scripture quotations are from The ESV Bible (The Holy Bible, English Standard Version) copyright 2001 by Crossway, a publishing Ministry of Good News Publishers. Used by permission. All rights reserved.

Balboa Press books may be ordered through booksellers or by contacting:

Balboa Press
A Division of Hay House
1663 Liberty Drive
Bloomington, IN 47403
www.balboapress.com
1 (877) 407-4847

Because of the dynamic nature of the Internet, any web addresses or links contained in this book may have changed since publication and may no longer be valid. The views expressed in this work are solely those of the author and do not necessarily reflect the views of the publisher, and the publisher hereby disclaims any responsibility for them.

The author of this book does not dispense medical advice or prescribe the use of any technique as a form of treatment for physical, emotional, or medical problems without the advice of a physician, either directly or indirectly. The intent of the author is only to offer information of a general nature to help you in your quest for emotional and spiritual well-being. In the event you use any of the information in this book for yourself, which is your constitutional right, the author and the publisher assume no responsibility for your actions.

Any people depicted in stock imagery provided by Thinkstock are models, and such images are being used for illustrative purposes only. Certain stock imagery © Thinkstock.

Print information available on the last page.

ISBN: 978-1-5043-8249-6 (sc)
ISBN: 978-1-5043-8250-2 (hc)
ISBN: 978-1-5043-8251-9 (e)

Library of Congress Control Number: 2017911881

Balboa Press rev. date: 08/26/2017

Contents

LOVE

Dedication

To Diana, love of my life,
author of happiness,
compass in this life's confusions,
companion in the next

Introduction

Come walk these roads with me. Some of the pavement is difficult, but stay light of heart. This book, like the life well lived, is full of whimsy. There is music and poetry. And being sort of an autobiography, that's how it should be.

More Introduction

A trinity informs our life. It gives our day shape and rhythm. The trinity of *politics, faith, and love*. You probably expected when I used the word "trinity" I would jump into some ambitious exegesis of the Christian triune God. But that is not what I am about.

No, I want you to recognize that as you live each day, your rhythms, your decisions, the flow of your day, all oscillate among these three great topics, these three great forces, even when you do not know it. Even if you have not thought about it until now, *politics, faith, and love* are the three forces of your life.

Without successful politics—that is, without the rational and orderly governance politics can provide, and does provide in most of the western world—we have severely reduced options in life. Art is not possible. Philosophy is not possible. Freedom to dissent is not possible. And dissent is perhaps the greatest privilege we have under a successful political system. Without good political governance, perhaps even feeding ourselves becomes a struggle.

Everything other than politics owes its life to politics. Everything is shaped by politics, for good or for ill. It is the air which sustains life or cheapens it.

Each of the three—*politics, faith, and love*—interacts with and influences the other two. Successful politics makes faith and love possible. (Yes, you can have a faith life and love your spouse under a despotism, even at Buchenwald, but I speak here mainly of conditions less dire.)

Faith gives politics its worthy purpose. Without faith, politics is a frantic exercise devoid of higher purpose. We do not recognize that God intervened in history at Bethlehem.

Without love, all of life is bleak. We are bereft individuals, sterile, drifting, alone. We have no human love and no Christ-given love. We do not recognize that God intervened at Bethlehem.

And so I write, looking back at thirteen years in academia, three years in law school, eight years of litigating as a lawyer, thirty-two years of conducting courtroom trials, and almost three blessed years of retirement.

I now see clearly that without successful, life-affirming politics no nation, even ours—the best and brightest political hope of mankind—can give its people the scope they need to flourish, the scope they need to pursue faith openly, freely, proudly. The scope to love each other openly, freely, proudly.

I see clearly that our recent politics of negation enervates the polity. Unresisted, it will destroy that polity. I see clearly that the 2017 politics of negation, in so-called "resistance" to our new president, is merely a trendy, easy course, a shallow substitute for thought, a vicious self-indulgence.

I see clearly that a nation without faith in its divine creator is just a drifting person writ large. It is a John Blake or a Nancy Jones blindly accomplishing tasks, blindly following a path someone said was valid.

I see clearly that without love of spouse, love of family, love of friends, love of country—without the given and received love of, yes, the triune God—we and our nation walk a barren path. A nation is just an individual writ large.

And so I urge you, dear reader, to entertain this construct of *politics, faith, and love* as the trinity that has been organizing your life. I have found it to be so in my life, and I posit that it is so in yours.

You may want to expand, you may want to loosen, your construct of "love" to include "enthusiasm." To live a life of love, a life of enthusiasm, is first to love others and be loved in turn; to love God and be loved in turn. [ENDNOTE 11] Second, to love is to be enthusiastic about many things in life.

For me, my enthusiasms are literature, writing, gardening, fishing, sporting clays, language, football, and figuring out how fiction writers tell their stories. That last thing is narrative technique, a love of mine, and the topic of my Ph.D. dissertation.

So, walk these roads with me. Experience the oscillation of my thought among these three forces, *politics, faith, and love*. I hope you find that this exhilarating oscillation inhabits your own life.

To set the stage, I give you some "musings" first. They are brief, but they will let you know better who I am, and the musings will help prepare you for the three separate sections which follow on *politics, faith, and love*.

MUSINGS

Chapter 1

SO, HOW DO YOU LIKE BEING RETIRED?

That's a question everybody asks a newly "retired" person. I get it a lot. I ask it myself when I meet someone who has just left his usual job description and not taken up something else yet. The answers are always interesting because every person is different.

No one has yet told me, "Oh, you know, I hate being retired. I don't know what to do with myself." But those people must exist. They must be around, because I do meet a lot of people who are "thinking of" retiring.

But those persons thinking of retiring tell me, "I don't think I will do it. I don't know what I would do with myself." Some of them surely must retire and then be unhappy. There must be a lot of former judges with post-retirement malaise, because the Tennessee Judicial Conference has periodic programs on postpartum depression.

When I get the question posed to me, I want to redefine it. I want the question to be, "How do you like not doing what you did for thirty-two years?" That's easy to answer: I love not doing what I did for thirty-two years. But in no sense do I consider myself "retired." I am just working in new areas. One of them is writing.

There are things I miss and don't miss about the judgeship of thirty-two years:

- I do not miss handling the busiest trial court of record in Tennessee. In the twelve months of 2013, my last full calendar year, I concluded 4,843 cases. (A "court of record" is one in which there is a record of the proceedings. In courts "not of record," oral proceedings are not recorded, and the judge makes his or her decision based on notes and memory. Circuit judge Rosenbalm's decision which you can read at the end of this book in ENDNOTE 2, was taken by a court reporter, and "put of record"—entered upon the minutes of the court—by the court clerk.)
- I do not miss talking to the jail at midnight to set bond and to schedule arraignments.
- I do not miss the lame excuses litigants give for man's inhumanity to man.
- I do not miss the sixty to seventy-hour work weeks—at court, in chambers, and at home—those hours absolutely necessary to handle incoming work. And I am sure my wonderful wife Diana does not miss those work weeks.
- I miss my great law clerks, who were then third-year law students from UT College of Law and Lincoln Memorial Law School—Elisabeth Bellinger, Jimmy Carter, Sharon Eun, John Higgins, Ryann Musick Jeffers, Holly Martin, Tina Osborn, Patrick Rose, Luke Shipley, Stephanie Epperson Stuart, Megan Swain.
- I miss the annual trial dockets Fourth Circuit held on the road at those two law schools, year after year, giving the entire student body—1Ls, 2Ls, and 3Ls—real courtrooms, three of them, all day long. Complete with prisoners and weeping litigants.

- I miss my wonderful court clerks, the Knox County employees who worked so hard to help domestic violence victims.
- I miss the best secretary in the world, Rachel. (An aside here: When I ever-so-slowly eased out her excellent predecessor, who had become with time not so excellent, Rachel's predecessor told me I would "rue the day" if I should replace her. I did not.)
- I miss seeing my attorney friends five days a week.
- I miss my many Special Masters, who served without pay every Thursday on domestic violence day, so that with three courts we could handle the docket load.
- I miss the domestic violence docket itself—that is, I miss the good work that the Special Masters, that Pat Bright, a gifted professional, and I did week after week. We complemented and amplified the excellent work of Legal Aid of East Tennessee, of the University of Tennessee nursing program, and of a host of fifty other professionals who saw a problem and rose to meet it.
- I miss being in a judgeship which has the power to help people (1) directly, (2) on schedule, (3) when they ask for it. Of course, even now I can and do help people through *pro bono* work and otherwise.
- And happily I anticipate opening a mediation practice in family law soon, where again I will be able to help people (1) directly, (2) on schedule, (3) when they ask for it.

Chapter 2

WHO ARE THE BEST PEOPLE? LAWYERS ARE THE BEST PEOPLE

Mary Kathleen Cunningham and I married in 1966. In 1972 Mary and I left Providence, Rhode Island, to enter law school in my home town, at the University of Tennessee George C. Taylor College of Law. We had a two-year-old boy in arms.

Mary worked very hard and made law review. I worked very hard and made *pater cum laude.* Mary eventually died of MS; my second marriage (but for two fine children and some great in-laws) was a mistake; and my third marriage has been twenty years of bliss and counting.

There is perhaps a fourth marriage, or maybe even more, which I will explain in a moment.

It was immediately clear to me the first day of law school that my fellow students were the best people in the world. Never in the previous thirteen years of academia had I encountered such joy of life, such spontaneous friendship. It continued through law school and into eight years' practice of law, and then through thirty-two years on the bench.

Lawyers are the best people in the world. And flexible: back then in law school, when we didn't have law licenses to lose, we often went to cock fights in South Knox County.

4

There we mixed with children and old men, talked with ladies from the auxiliary selling hotdogs and grilled cheese sandwiches for the church. And with young wives and sons-in-law, who were putting "two on the gray," or "five on the little red."

They were there for diversion, the society of friends, an evening off. They would break even, or win fifteen or lose fifteen. I like to think they were also there because they just would not be politically correct, would not buy the cultural imperialism of the sensitive elite. Would not tolerate being labeled rednecks, fools, misdemeanants, or as the newspaper liked to call them, consorters with drug dealers and mafiosi. "For the Lord's sake," I can imagine these good people saying, "It's the pennyrile pit in Lester's barn. Don't get your pants in a wad."

There are joys inherent in a judgeship, sure. Two stand out. The first is the ability always to do the right thing, the best thing, for the given facts of a case. The second is the continued association with the best and the brightest lawyers in East Tennessee from 1982 through 2014, the thirty-two years of being a circuit court judge.

I taught many years at the National Judicial College in Reno, Nevada; many years statewide for the Tennessee Judicial Conference; and many years for the Tennessee Bar Association and the Knoxville Bar Association. Teaching lawyers is far better than teaching judges. Practicing lawyers still have the joy of life, while we judges tend to be a bit *verklemmt*—I guess "wedged" is the best English for the German word describing a constrained attitude toward life.

Of course, having your home shot up, being stalked, and being threatened in social media and otherwise are pretty good reasons to end up wedged. That's why you won't find my children or grandchildren in my writings by name or town.

And then there's the running for public office. I like to say I have three doctorates—a Yale Ph.D. (German Literature), my beloved J.D. from the University of Tennessee George C. Taylor

School of Law, and a third doctorate in Elected Office Politics (EOP).

After four campaigns for those eight-year terms, my EOP degree comprises more hours of intense learning than formal training ever did. And it gave me a fourth wife, and possibly even more. (An election opponent, David Lee, accused me of concealing various divorces from multiple wives, one of whom was definitively stated to be "Kathy", a nurse.

I have searched throughout Tennessee for Kathy and been unable to find her, but she lives happily in Swann family mythology. Kathy is responsible for many of my omissions and errors. Indeed, if you don't have a Kathy in your home life, you probably should invent one.

The experience of the judgeship was the ultimate impetus for my 2016 book *Five Proofs of Christianity*. You can read much of it for free at www.amazon.com/author/judgebillswann. Seeing so many lives pass before me, in 1985 I saw that I needed to figure out where I stood as to Christianity. The little 2016 book is my take on that. If my journey interests you, or if you wonder about your personal take on Christianity, or indeed whether you should bother with Christianity at all, you will enjoy my meandering reflections.

The book you are now holding deals with many things, among them local Knox County elected politics as seen from the perspective of an EOP degree holder. I hope this second book is both funny and serious. My thirteen years as a German academic informs much of the serious content of these two books—a different perspective on life than most people have.

Parenthetically, I maintain that an advanced (real) degree in any subject matter is great preparation for the practice of law. Why? Because knowing a different set of meticulous, demanding criteria helps you be relaxed about the arcane depths of legalisms.

But I do not pine away for my lost contacts with attorneys. Because soon I will begin a mediation practice devoted to family law, and once again I will have daily contact with the best people. I will limit the mediation to my expertise of thirty-two years; price my hourly for accessibility; and bring a judicial perspective to the process of "getting to yes."

I look forward eagerly to being with my lawyer friends again. Of course, we cannot get together in South Knox County: Having law degrees now, we cannot go to cock fights.

Chapter 3

RICHARD, AGE 19

Not long ago I tried a case with a nineteen-year-old witness. Let's call him Richard. He had grown up in housing projects, and had just gotten out of jail. His older brother was still in state prison; his younger sister had become a mother at age twelve. Richard testified about his juvenile and adult convictions for car theft, burglary, and criminal impersonation.

But the picture wasn't right. He was articulate, had a large vocabulary. He was clearly intelligent. He had done well in school, very well, until the ninth grade. Then it had all fallen apart. Happily, the lawyer doing the direct examination asked exactly what I wanted to ask: "Richard, what went wrong in the ninth grade?"

He said, "Man, let me tell you smart don't get it. I mean, it's great and all that when you're a kid, and you're at the blackboard, and you've got the answer, and the teacher says, 'Very good, Richard.' But then you go back to your seat, and the cool kids are saying, 'Look at him, he's a nerd!'"

"I wanted to be like the cool kids. They were happy and everything. They were all stealing stuff. I wanted to be like them. So I started stealing stuff too."

Maybe this young man was just blowing smoke. It's entirely

possible. Judges get a lot of smoke. But I thought of myself going into the ninth grade. [ENDNOTE 8] It was September 1956.

Webb School had started the year before, 1955, with four students. I sat there on the bench looking at Richard, a judge in my black robe, and wondered what would have become of him if he had been able to go to private school in the ninth grade. In 1956 I got to go to a school where learning was cool. Not stealing, not drugs. Where everyone had the same goal, to learn as much as possible. By age nineteen, Richard's age, I was in my second year of college.

What if Richard had been saved from his public school environment, as I was, plucked up, rescued? Well, Richard would still have been nineteen, but he would have been in college on a big scholarship. Because he was smart and well-spoken and a hard worker. He might even have had a clean record.

So, what's my point? Mr. Webb changed my life. He gave me the chance to excel. He made me successful. Without him, there wouldn't have been three straight years of his Latin instruction, no Ted Bruning for English, no George Turley for math, no B.E. Sharp for football. Mr. Webb put it all together—his school, and my life.

Too bad he didn't have a shot at doing that for Richard.

Chapter 4

DREAMS

Let's turn for a bit to things more nebulous. Dreams. These often scary experiences fit ultimately, as I hope you will also find, in the category of faith.

I have recurrent dreams of Harvard College. You too may have recurrent dreams, troubling dreams, ones you need to deal with seriously. Perhaps my experience can help.

In my recurring departure from reality, what I call "Dream One," there are contiguous Cambridge streets which form shifting parallelograms displacing themselves around Dunster Street, like a Stephen King folding map ("*Mrs. Todd's Shortcut,*" 1984).

I cannot get from Harvard Yard to Kirkland House. I keep trying. The streets don't connect as they should. I end up on Memorial Drive. I start over. Same result. Memorial Drive. Yes, there's the Charles River. But sometimes pieces of the Yale campus intrude as I try to walk from the Yard to Kirkland. This does not surprise me in the dream. Sometimes it's so bad I can't even find Harvard Square, which is silly, because for a year I lived there, across the street from The Harvard Coop.

This is simply—says a drugstore psychologist—that I am out of place at Harvard. I am unworthy. I don't belong there. "They"— that's the capital "They"—will find out soon and send me back home, back to Tennessee. Back to where I belong. More my speed.

The dream is my lecture to myself, my galloping insecurity. On the other hand, maybe not. Maybe this is evil intervening in my life.

The second of the lost dreams, "Dream Two," involves test-taking at Harvard. In real life I always test well. But not in Dream Two. I am in the largest Harvard testing venue, Memorial Hall, taking an exam for a course I have never attended. (To my joy I later learned that hundreds of Harvard alumni have this dream.)

A variant of the dream, "Dream Three," a wickedly haunting version, is that I am enrolled for a normal Harvard load, four courses, but I don't know what they are. I cannot find out what they are. I cannot correct this situation, because I cannot get to University Hall (see Dream One) to find out what I registered for.

A variant on "Dream Three" is that I cannot get inside University Hall to see the posted reading lists for courses I might be in, so that at least I can buy the books at the Coop in Harvard Square (if I can get there) and read them. If I could just get close to University Hall, maybe I could ask someone what I was registered for. That someone could go in and read the posting for me, and then come out and tell me.

I stand outside, like poor Josef K. in Kafka's *Trial*, trying to find out what he is accused of doing.

Dreams One, Two, and Three, and their variants—says the drugstore psychologist—are clear statements that I am intellectually inadequate to the task of performing at Harvard. And yes, that "They" will soon find out, and send me back home. Back to Tennessee. Back to where I belong.

Needless to say after nights like these, I wake up tired and full of self doubt. What joy, The Eastern Education.

Chapter 5

RACCOONS, OKRA,
AND SQUASH

No sane thinking person, I hope, inflicts pain upon another sentient being. On the other hand, if raccoons and possums are killing your chickens, you must kill them. Trap them and kill them. Relocation does not work. I've tried it.

The problem with the killing is, when you take your .22 pistol and shoot a raccoon or possum in the head, it takes him thirty seconds of flopping around to bleed out and lie still. If you shoot him again, or even a third time, thinking he is in pain, it still takes the full thirty seconds from the first shot. No short cuts. It's not that the .22 is underpowered. A .38 gets the same thirty-second drama.

After forty-one raccoons and ten possums, I have concluded they are all dead after one shot, and that the drama is autonomic musculature. No pain. I hope. My authority is the chicken herself: Beheaded, she is instantly dead, but the body still runs around for thirty seconds, bumping into things. It's enough to make you a vegetarian.

On the other hand, growing okra is foolproof. Put the seed in the ground, and up it comes, eventually reaching six feet tall, pods everywhere. As in *The Fantasticks*, "Plant a Radish, Get a Radish."

But growing squash is not foolproof. The squash vine borer is a small beast from hell. In the month of July 2016 he defeated me for the sixth and last time. I will not plant squash again in Tennessee. He has won. He cannot be bested by chemicals, by crop rotation, or by shooting him in the head with a pistol.

If I can catch a squash vine borer, I will send him to Harvard and make him wander about lost with no reading list.

Chapter 6

PLAYING THE LUTE

All this pondering on Harvard and personal inadequacy begs for its opposing bookend, some sort of optimistic pondering on "The Life Well Lived," or something hopeful like that.

Years ago the urge to fight back spurred me to write a tiny poem. I asked: "How can I be, if not excellent, at least adequate in the face of overwhelming odds, the explosion of knowledge, the need to keep up?"

On Being Unable to Play the Lute

I cannot play the lute.
The fact that my neighbor
Also cannot play the lute
Is of no moment.
The point is, you see,
I will never know luteness.
Oh yes, I could, as you say,
Take lessons in lute.
I could remove this flaw
To my completeness.
But I won't.

It's because, it's because, well,
There are too many instruments now.
Time has marched on.
Pico della Mirandola had only one lute.
Now lutes have been squared and cubed.
Braqued and Picassoed and Einsteined.
Who can play them all?

Oh, once it was enough
To play the lute and ride the horse,
Write poetry,
Sing, throw a few stones.
Life was simple,
All knowledge could be mastered.
But not now.

Do you think I could just, well,
Get a little place somewhere
And maybe wind lute strings?
Something simple,
Something within my grasp,
Something, you know, finite?
I could put the strings
In little glassine bags.
Maybe I could do that.
Yeah, maybe that.

This of course is not really a poem about music. It is about the absence of all those individual perfections which lie beyond my grasp. Too many to name in my case, but one missing for me is in fact luteness. I am musically ungifted. I have tried to become competent on the banjo and acoustic bass, but to no happy end. I have no rhythm. Frets are not my friend.

I was marched through piano lessons as a child. They did not take. I can play some harmonica, because it stays on pitch and has no frets. As the saying goes, I can play the radio.

Yet I love music. My ear is good. I can sing a passable second tenor if I am standing next to a really good second tenor. My listening tastes run from plainchant through Bach to Arrowsmith to Keith Jarrett and Kelly Joe Phelps. I can see the promised land, but I cannot enter it.

Chapter 7

DREAMS AGAIN

Dreams One, Two, and Three above, as I said, are recurring dreams. "Dream Four" occurred last night. That was the first time for Dream Four. And once is enough. The basics are the same—Cambridge again. I can't get where I want to go. [ENDNOTE SIX] I am lost in a familiar setting, that is, lost where there is no logic to the lostness But the streets I am walking are totally familiar to me. I know each one, where it interlocks with the next, or is supposed to, what a right or left turn should lead to. But they do not. I have memories of things which happened on those streets. I know where Elsie's Sandwich Shop is. I am, in short, not really lost.

But yet I am, because my individual streets do not interlock, do not constitute a whole. Just as a disassembled jigsaw puzzle scattered upon a table makes no overall sense, but yet you know there is sense behind it, a sense to be made of it, a use to which to put those pieces, still you cannot make a cogent whole just looking at the pieces.

You are lost. The terror I feel in a nightmare is the greater because I see the potential of the puzzle pieces but cannot make the joinings. Because of that failing, in the midst of the dream I doubt my sanity, the greatest terror of all.

I once had a similar thing happen fully awake. It was in a multi-level parking garage. You know where this is going. I had come in on one level (*Now just which entrance was it?*), parked on another level (*It was up, wasn't it, from where I drove in?*), re-entered the garage on foot on a third and different level (*maybe*), and had a picture in my head (*sort of*) of what the parking slot looked like (*The truck is facing out, isn't it?*).

The disorientation came, of course, from not carefully paying attention at each step earlier. It did not come from insanity. But the disorientation was just as profound.

Well, the Stephen King Cambridge streets joined themselves last night to technology. In last night's dream, Dream Four, I was lost in Cambridge again, oh yes. But this time I know what to do. No problem—I have a cell phone. I can call University Hall and ask for directions.

But first I need the telephone number for University Hall. It turns out unfortunately that Cambridge (all Boston? all Massachusetts? the whole world?) has no 411 service. I punch in 411, and the phone does nothing. I punch in zero for the operator and get a nice young woman who is not the phone company. She is a private citizen. I try 411 again and this time 411 works, but I get the same nice young lady. I don't have any other numbers or persons to call, and at this point my phone becomes very thin and slim, and I misplace it in one of my very many pockets. I can't find my phone. My head is aching, and I wake up, out of the dream, but still terrified.

This dream is not good. It is taking on a life of its own. This dream of Cambridge, like the small extraterrestrial precursor in Ridley Scott's 1979 *Alien*, is morphing into something larger. Things are going to get worse. All technology is against me. What is to come next? If the cell phone is to stay in the dream, perhaps the next escalation is that the buttons on the phone become so small that I cannot use them.

Chapter 8

DREAMS YET AGAIN

Our worst nightmares may be glimpses of personal insanity. They may be trial runs into a complete loss of bearings, trial runs into a complete loss of control, a surrender to the rising panic that we may never find our way out of this particular dilemma. These nightmares change as they go. They metamorphose ever onward, presenting new difficulties, ever new barriers which—when surmounted—are followed by yet other barriers.

One of those new barriers is often a stranger in that horrid land, upon whom we lean for guidance and who himself is fallible and confused. He gives us faulty advice in the dream. But no matter, then we see a landmark that says, "This way, this way is home."

And so with relief we conclude, "Well, it seems to be so. That really is the landmark we remember, isn't it? That is Ayres Hall, isn't it?"

Yes, and so we remember that Ayres Hall is on the way to Circle Park. Isn't that right? Being unsure, we ask someone else, and that someone says, "No, you don't want to go in that direction. You want to go this way," which is 180 degrees from where we were headed. So what to do now? Take the new direction, the 180-degree direction?

Well, that's a plan of action. Let's try it. Something is better than nothing. But then our bowels, or lust, or our urinary tract—one of them—asserts itself in the dream and that becomes the primary need, not the new 180-degree direction.

And then just at that juncture another someone appears, a person we know from the real world, who causes new problems in the dream. These new problems are not of direction, but derivations of the problems the new someone really does cause us, has caused us in the real world. So now we have to deal with this real person while we are still thoroughly lost as to direction, and still worried about bowels-lust-urine.

If this nightmare is not a glimpse of personal insanity, it is a good strong run at it. Or a foretaste of hell. The nightmare has no solution. There is no resolution, no way out, no "Aha! That path over there is the path to sunlight and buttercups." No, that never happens. The best we can do is wake up and wonder just what all that mess was about.

It leaves a bad taste. Part of the bad taste, of course, is the recognition that we ourselves are the stereopticon producing this slide show. Unless perhaps it is produced by evil, by the prowling lion of 1 Peter 5, which as I age seems ever more possible:

> *Your adversary the devil prowls around like a roaring lion, seeking someone to devour. Resist him, firm in your faith, knowing that the same kinds of suffering are being experienced by your brotherhood throughout the world.*
>
> *1 Peter 5: 8-9*

But the good news amongst this bad is this: If indeed a force of evil is the projectionist behind this sad entertainment, then we are off the responsibility hook. We didn't cook up this mess of insanity from our own fevered brains. The lion did. The evil lion. He controls us, much as the ghost of Hamlet's murdered father takes over Hamlet's mind:

I could a tale unfold whose lightest word
Would harrow up thy soul, freeze thy young blood,
Make thy two eyes, like stars, start from their
spheres,
Thy knotted and combined locks to part
And each particular hair to stand on end,
Like quills upon the fretful porpentine: . . .
Act 1, Scene 5

We are harrowed by the nightmare the lion causes, just as Hamlet is harrowed by hearing the cause of his father's death. But the lion does not give us truth. Oh no, he gives us an imagined hell exquisitely and exactly tailored just for us.

But the good news, as I say, is that we don't have to own this manufactured mess of potage. It is a pile of slop the lion dumped on our plate. He wanted to see what we would do, how we would handle it. Or, being the force of evil, he just wants us to suffer.

But whoever the projectionist is—whether we are running the show or the lion is—things are not well. At the very least, we didn't handle it well last night. We didn't, for example, recognize the faint beeping of the dream as it began. We didn't hear the garbage truck backing slowly into our life, full of dread, full of remembered mistakes, past enemies, hopeless dilemmas. No, we let the dream continue until hopelessness overwhelmed us.

Authorship is important. If we are the authors of this slide show, then there is work to do.

How about counseling? (*Might work, but probably of little real help.*) Psychoanalysis? (*Once all the rage, now a discredited path.*) What about talk with a good friend? (*Well, it might be good for us, but it won't be good for him. And he might conclude—oh, woe—and even say, "Yes, you are crazy."*)

Well, how about drugs or alcohol to prevent dreams? I had a friend in New Haven who used J.W. Dant 100 proof and soda to do this, and yes, there was abatement, but at a huge cost to his body and well being. Still, he slept well . . .

So, we are left with the best of all options: contemplation nested in prayer. Whether we are the author-projectionist or the lion is running the show, we only need to give this mess to God and ask for help.

My faith journey started—you may remember this from *Five Proofs of Christianity* (Westbow Press, 2016)—with my need to know what (if anything at all) was real about Christ and the assurance of peace. This was in Reno, Nevada, in 1984 at the National Judicial College.

I thought I remembered an assurance of peace was somewhere in the New Testament. I knew it was often in the dismissal of Episcopal worship. What, if anything, was all that about? Just blather? Just words? Or for real?

Well, if the assurance of peace was truly there, and if it was truly real, then it was indeed everything. Then it was the answer to all earthly woes actual and imagined. So I read avidly in the gospels in 1984, searching. I learned that Christ did not say, "I will give you peace from your bad dreams. Come unto me and I will stop your Cambridge nightmares." He said far more than that. One of the things he said was:

> *Peace I leave with you; my peace I give to you. Not as the world gives do I give to you. Let not your hearts be troubled, neither let them be afraid.*
> *John 14:27*

So if you, like me, cannot hear the beep-beep of the garbage truck backing into your dreams, come with me and read again the three synoptic gospels (Matthew, Mark, and Luke) and the book of John. And hear with me the Episcopal dismissal from Philippians 4:7:

The Peace of God, which passeth all understanding, keep your hearts and minds in the knowledge and love of God, and of his Son Jesus Christ our Lord: And the Blessing of God Almighty, the Father, the Son, and the Holy Ghost, be amongst you and remain with you always. Amen.

Chapter 9

MOVING TO TENNESSEE

I was almost seven when my parents told me we were moving from Boston to Knoxville. It was the summer of 1949. [ENDNOTE 8] They told me we would have a moving van. When it came, it was a huge Mayflower van, green and yellow. I sat on the front lawn with the dandelions and watched the loading.

My cat, Mittens, made the move to Tennessee. He is the cat in the chapter "It Is What It Is". I was in the back seat of our Ford coupe with Mittens on the back deck behind me, sleeping in the sun on a blanket. This was the "Indian blanket" beloved of the family. All was fine until the Bal-Wash tunnel, which distressed Mittens, causing him to miaou loudly and blow his bowels all over the blanket. The stench was amazing. *"Aargh!"* bellowed my father. Driving with one hand, he reached behind, across me, seized the Indian blanket, and flung it out the window. When you are six years old, such becomes the stuff of legend.

Knoxville was because of black lung. My father hired on as an associate to a doctor with a nascent and booming surgery practice. Kentucky miners coming south to the big city of Knoxville for surgery. Lung resections. Respiratory therapy. My father lasted six months as an associate, found out he didn't like taking orders, and opened his own practice.

My father had decided to change from obstetrics to chest

surgery in China during the war, while part of a Mobile Army Surgical Hospital [ENDNOTE 8]. It was known as a CBI Unit (China-Burma-India theater) and is written up this way in the history of CBI units:

> The 22nd Field Hospital was activated at Camp White, Ore., on Aug. 1, 1942. The original cadre under command of 1st Lt. William K. Swann, Jr., and 22 enlisted men originated from Bradley Field, Windsor Locks, Conn.
>
> To complete the T/O, officers and enlisted men were sent from all parts of the country . . .
>
> In January 1943 it became evident that the unit was to be composed partly of American Chinese, Officers of Chinese descent, and American officers who had had considerable experience in China, and large groups of American Chinese enlisted personnel were transferred to the organization.
>
> On Nov. 20, 1942, Lt. Col. Willis D. Butler assumed command of the organization, relieving 1st Lt. Swann.
>
> Following a short review of basic training, an advanced training program was instituted. This consisted of motor convoys, road marches, defenses against chemical warfare, field sanitation, emergency treatment of the sick and wounded on the field, setting up of hospital tents, advance course in ward nursing, etc.
>
> www.cbi-history.com

Family mythology states that a tiger mauling was involved in my father's conversion to chest surgery. There is a photograph of a mangled villager brought to the MASH. My father often performed chest surgery on injured Chinese at the Field Hospital.

What is not mythology but firm family lore is my father's own delighted account of shaving in the surgical tent in China. It was hot. My father would strip to the waist and shave his face with the assistance of his Chinese orderly. My father had heavy chest hair. Chinese soldiers avidly watched this every day, gesturing and repeating a particular word. After some days my father asked his orderly what that word meant. "Monkey," said the orderly.

15 February 1961 my father put a pacemaker in Mary Gentry's chest. She was twenty-six. [ENDNOTE 8] In 1961 Mary was the world's youngest pacemaker recipient. In 2012 she became the world's oldest (living) pacemaker recipient. In 2012 Mary showed me pictures of the daughter conceived and born after the pacemaker, the daughter who never would have been born otherwise. Mary's daughter became a fashion model for L.L. Bean catalogs.

Chapter 10

CHRISTMAS WHEN
YOU WERE SEVEN

What were you thinking of at Christmas in 1949 when you were seven? Or if you were not seven in 1949—but in 1969 or 1989—what were you thinking? Thoughts of Santa Claus? Thoughts of gifts to come?

You probably were not thinking about the gifts you were giving, or could give, because you weren't giving any. Not at seven. You were still in the receiving mode, a child. A blissful child—with some worries, yes. The family is frightening at times, yes. But you are able to wash all that away with the smell of balsam and the magic of Christmas tree lights.

You lie under the tree and look up through the branches. In 1949 you saw and smelled the hot, pointed, in-series lights. The kind that when one burns out the whole string goes dark. Then it was your job to find the burned-out bulb and restore the tree to glory. No such problem in 1969 or 1989: If one bulb burns out, the rest of the string is fine because it is wired in parallel.

There was an electric train in 1949. I wager that you cannot remember your seven-year-old Christmas. I remember the tree, those lights, the train, and Christmas carols—the first I had ever heard—at school [ENDNOTE 8]:

He thought of children, tiered and glowing,
Standing on stair steps reaching
All the way to heaven,
Reaching so high the air was thin and shimmering
Where the oldest stood, singing,
Singing in the school's foyer,
Singing Oh, little town,
He thought of children, tiered and glowing,
Singing with no fear of megaliths
Falling, white-crusted, waves driven asunder,
Gulls sent screaming,
Their wingtips slapping foam.

The story of the baby Jesus was nice, oh yes. It seemed like a fairy tale then, a story which we heard at Christmas. The little town of Bethlehem was a long way off, that was for sure, farther even than Etowah or Dalton.

If you can remember your Christmas at age seven, look under your glowing memories and see what uneasiness was there for you—denied perhaps, glanced away from—in the grandeur of Christmas. Maybe your only happiness other than Christmas was school, or playing with your cat. Or one real orange. Maybe you were afraid, even then.

SCHOOL, 1949-1952

The boy threw up on the way to school,
Regularly,
A matter of course,
Compass-setting.
The stink of decomposing plankton
Would rise into his blowholes,
And make his bright eyes water,
Make the sidewalk swim.

His almost hairless body, half-formed,
Wet cetacean eyes casting about,
Sought protection, not ritual heaves,
Not emesis on neighborhood lawns.

His mother protected him when she could,
Let him swim in her shadow,
Helped him feed, hid him
When she herself was not in danger,
The denouncéd whore, the common slut,
The bright-eyed nurse.

He scraped his way along the sidewalks
Thinking six times nine, four times three,
Thinking bile-tinged thoughts.
He thought of the school cafeteria, steaming,
Waiting, windows fogged,
A place that sometimes had no food for whales.
He thought of home and crashing waves,
The leaping thrashing father,
Up, up into bright air,
Leaping high and falling back into the sea,
Killing what lay below him,
Denouncing the whore.

He wondered how it could be
That at home only she loved him,
Only his mother,
While at school many, many loved him.
Even the ladies in the cafeteria,
Even on the days
When there was no food for whales.

He thought of children, tiered and glowing,
Standing on stair steps reaching
All the way to heaven,
Reaching so high the air was thin and shimmering
Where the oldest stood, singing,
Singing in the school's foyer,
Singing Oh, little town,
Singing with no fear of megaliths
Falling, white-crusted, waves driven asunder,
Gulls sent screaming,
Their wingtips slapping foam.

He thought of his teacher who loved him,
Who loved his gray skin,
His smooth gray skin,
Who gave him stamps and stars.
At night, rising to breathe,
He saw her stars among the stars,
Her stamped cat shapes upon the constellations.
At night, rising to breathe,
He knew he wanted to live in school,
Wanted to breathe the dust of tempera paints
And construction paper forever,
Far from falling fear,
Far from barnacled screams.
He knew he wanted to live, and live, and live,
Without bile, without flukes,
Beyond the horizon, among the stars.

Well, we all grow up, scared or not. We move on, become responsible adults. Achieve. Help others. Find faith. Weep. But the wonder of that first remembered Christmas remains. Sweet, sweet, magical. Bitter sweet.

Chapter 11

ACROPHOBIA

In 1964 acrophobia was just a tickling, an uneasiness. It happened in the gentle ridges of Styria in Austria. I was living with an Austrian family, spending a year as a Fulbright exchange student in Graz [ENDNOTE 8], "die Stadt der Volkserhebung." (Graz had been one of Hitler's favorite towns, the first town in Austria to hoist the swastika flag.) My Austrian brother and I were hiking over ridge lines. Going up was fine. Going down was not. Like A.A. Milne's Tigger in the tree:

> *Roo was silent for a little while, and then he said, "Shall we eat our sandwiches, Tigger?" And Tigger said, "Yes, where are they?" And Roo said, "At the bottom of the tree." And Tigger said, "I don't think we'd better eat them just yet." So they didn't . . .*
> *"Hallo, Roo," called Piglet. What are you doing?"*
> *"We can't get down, we can't get down!" cried Roo. "Isn't it fun? Pooh, isn't it fun, Tigger and I are living in a tree, like Owl, and we're going to stay here for ever and ever. I can see Piglet's house. Piglet, I can see your house from here. Aren't we high? Is Owl's house as high up as this?"*
> *"How did you get there, Roo?" asked Piglet.*

"On Tigger's back! And Tiggers can't climb downwards, because their tails get in the way, only upwards, and Tigger forgot about that when we started, and he's only just remembered. So we've got to stay here for ever and ever—unless we go higher. What did you say, Tigger? Oh, Tigger says if we go higher we shan't be able to see Piglet's house so well, so we're going to stop here."
"Piglet," said Pooh solemnly, when he had heard all this, "what shall we do?" And he began to eat Tigger's sandwiches.
—The House at Pooh Corner, 1928

Five years later my acrophobia reached maturity. I was on spring break from Berlin, 1969, traversing a steep slope with my ski instructor. Nothing difficult. Then I looked down to the right, down and down over the thick, rigid snow crust to jagged rocks far below. If I should fall, I realized, I would slide on top of the thick crust, faster and faster. If I slid, I would die. I could not move.

It was good to get back to Berlin, to deal with literature and political problems.

Chapter 12

MOUNT LECONTE, THE BERLIN WALL, AND THREE WEEKS OF PRE-MED

Mt. Katahdin in Maine, 5270 feet high, is the first place in the United States touched by the rising sun. Some heretics say, no, it is Mars Hill or Mount Cadillac. But I know better. My grandfather Young and I hiked it in 1959.

At 6593 feet above sea level, Tennessee's Mt. LeConte is the _tallest_ mountain in the eastern United States. It is completely in Tennessee. It is a sudden and solitary offshoot of the main Appalachian crest which forms the state boundary with North Carolina. LeConte is a magnificent mountain, my home for the summer of 1961.

"Tall" refers to the rise of a mountain from base to crest. Mt. Mitchell in North Carolina is the _highest_ mountain east of the Mississippi, 6684 feet, but it is not the _tallest_. Gatlinburg, Tennessee, elevation 1453 feet, lies at the foot of Mt. LeConte.

I hiked that 5140-foot difference twenty times the summer of 1961, as a part of my job as fire layer, bed maker, table server, and general step-and-fetch-it for LeConte Lodge. The lodge was a forty-three-guest concession just below the top of the mountain. It was a great job. It seemed impossible I should get paid for it. Fifty dollars a week. I had to get a social security number. I was against it. I thought it was awful that the government gave its citizens a number. But I did want the money. Situational ethics.

"Boys," Herrick Brown told Alan and me, the other step-and-fetch-it, "you've got to stop pissing out the cabin door. See all those butterflies?" And thus I learned that butterflies like urine.

Alan was Appalachian by birth; I became an Appalachian by adoption. Alan dislocated his shoulder twice that summer and pulled it back into place with his other arm. He killed a bear that summer, chasing it for hours through the woods. He rode a guest's horse bareback, with me behind him holding on, one mile out the shale-clattering, narrow, Myrtle Point trail and back. A five-hundred foot drop on the left going out, the same on the right coming back, once we could turn around. That was three years before I discovered acrophobia.

LeConte was the summer of the Berlin Wall, 13 August 1961, the summer after my freshman year of college [ENDNOTE 8]. We had no newspaper and no radio on Mt. LeConte. I learned of the wall from two German lodge guests. It seemed to me an oddity, nothing more. What was important to me was not the wall, not politics, but that I got to speak German with the German guests.

It was at Harvard that I discovered I was good in foreign languages. Until then, I had had only Latin, three years of it. The first week in Cambridge I asked my freshman roommate what modern language to take, because I had to take something—there was a foreign language requirement at Harvard then—and he said I should take either Russian or German because I was pre-med. I said I didn't care. He said, well, German then, because he had liked Switzerland when he was there. So I took German.

The pre-med lasted only three weeks. Math was a requirement for pre-med.

I did not understand even the vocabulary in Harvard's beginning math course. I dutifully went to all the section meetings, studied the book, met with the T.A. three times in office hours. "Bill," said the T.A., "I think you should consider dropping this course." I did, and sold my textbook back to The Coop.

The German, however, took root and flowered. As did Spanish, senior year. I learned to read French in graduate school—a requirement for my Ph.D. degree—by reading James Bond novels. It is embarrassing how easy languages are for me. But not Harvard beginning math.

In 1989 the wall came down. It lasted from 1961 to 1989. My son born in 1970 brought me a piece of it, the son who went to law school with Mary and me. The wall was a failed government program. One that lasted twenty-eight years. The United states has had daylight savings time some fifty-one years [ENDNOTE 9], also a failed (but evidently permanent) government program. The people of East Germany, not their government, ended the program.

Chapter 13

"IT IS WHAT IT IS."

A cat, a radio, an electric train, and a wagon. Four simple things. Not much content, not much meat, for the poem below. Well, five things. The Lone Ranger is in there too. Still sounds pretty thin, doesn't it? Let's see if my poem works:

1918-20 West Clinch Avenue,
Knoxville Winter 1949

1
It was a house that winters smelled of trains—
Of ozone, dust, transformer windings.
A house that smelled of grimy panes,
Of flaking sills and heavy blindings,
Of casements gritty, dust of coal,
The smell of trains, James Agee's trains,
The L&N nine blocks away.
It was a house that summers smelled of rains
Of clean-washed sills, a streaming walk,
Of rains which washed the back stoop clean,
Which made the rooms feel warm, protected,
Safe from death both in and out.

2

Here dwelled a boy who lived in smells,
Deep morning smells upon the ridge,
The smell of clinkers, scuttle pails,
The smell of coal upon the ridge,
The ridge where General Sanders died.

3

He was a boy deep lost in trains—
He was not happy, only lost—
His boxcars rattling, storm-blown reeds.
He'd stop his train at times and breathe,
Draw in the ash smell, heavy musk,
Draw in the ozone born of sparks,
Hold close his Lionel, black and cold,
Hold close its mass, cold bas relief.
My train's from far away, he thought,
Meteor-heavy, cannot stay,
It cannot stay here, cannot stay,
Down here on carpet thin and gray.

4

His engine hauled its cars
Round clattery tracks so fast
That sections would disjoin—roll out—
Go thump! the engine would,
A solid, sidewise thumping roll.
A .38 laid down with force.
The boy would sit there, listen, smell,
Breathe in the ozone, carpet dust—
Breathe in the heated windings' smell,
And know he had the winter's smell.

5

Inside the Stromberg radio—
His parents' pride, great ponderous thing,
Brown wooden console, glowing light—
Inside the radio, things died, sure,
But not so much as could have been.
Stromberg-Carlson was his world
Three times a week at half-past six.
Inside the radio, things died, yes,
But not so much as might have been:
It was, in all, a sunny place
Because the Ranger shot so well.
He shot the guns from outlaws' hands.
Sometimes he shot them in the arms.
Sometimes they shot him in the flesh.

6

Outside the Stromberg, things died, sure:
At summer's end, the butterflies,
Pale paper wings, pale dusty sheets,
Stiff and falling back and forth,
Back and forth down through the air.
No noise then, no, just whispers then,
Down through the air, down to the ground.

7

The boy's gray cat, though, did not die,
Not summer's end, not winter's start.
He just went off to find his heart,
Or chase the catbirds—that was it!—
Or maybe, maybe, went Up High,
Went there to play, play all day long.
That's where he was, yes, probably.

8

Beside the house there, in the cool,
Between the hedge and back stoop wall,
There, where the shade and water ran,
Where summers it was good to play,
The boy's cat watched him building dams,
Before he went away to stay,
Before he went away to play,
Up High, and left the boy alone.

9

His mother did not die then, no,
Not at the end of summer, no.
She did not die then, never would,
She'd never leave him: she was good.
Nor did his father die then, no—
Self-blind figure wrapped in fear—
No washing him down hose-gush path,
No downhill sluice in creamy chert,
No roiling pebbles, foaming clay.
No, not so easy: He would stay.

10

The far side of the house was vast,
The duplex side, a cold grass field,
The side that ran on towards the Fort,
Where Sanders got the shoulder wound,
Where, at the top, he could push off,
Left knee bent in, right leg crooked out,
And pump down hard, pump fast, and push,
Push down hard and tuck both legs:
Clattery, noisy, cold downhill.

11

He'd hold the cold black tongue, hold tight,
Not roll and spill until was right,
Stay inside his storm blown reeds,
World a-tremble, thin gray carpet,
'Til the tongue-lash time would come,
'Til turning hard he'd spill the wagon,
Fall out fast, disjoin, and slide.
Cold bitter sea: slide, roll, and laugh,
A solid, sidewise thumping roll,
Six-chambered cylinder smooth and cold,
See gray sky whirl, and hospital—
The one they gave the General's name—
And laugh until rotation stopped.

This poem—any poem, any novel, any play—"is what it is." By that hopeless cliché, I mean it is self-contained. You hold it in your hand. It is an artistic whole.

Who the author is doesn't matter. Who he was—where he lived; what he said about monarchy, marriage, or Irish independence; whether he was handsome or ugly; all that lies outside the artifact, the thing you hold in your hand. We are to concern ourselves— thus says New Criticism—only with the work at hand. Explicate it, grasp it, reflect upon it, stay within it.

New Criticism is one of the fairly recent swings of the lit-crit pendulum. It is useful in many ways, not the least of which is its simplicity. We are not burdened, for example, by the knowledge that T.S. Eliot was an anti-Semite as we read in the first lines of "The Wasteland":

> *Summer surprised us, coming over the*
> *Starnbergersee*
> *With a shower of rain; we stopped in the colonnade,*
> *And went on in sunlight, into the Hofgarten,*

> *And drank coffee, and talked for an hour.*
> *Bin gar keine Russin, stamm' aus Litauen, echt*
> *deutsch.*

That phrase, 'true German,' will have a different resonance if we take a biographical approach to *"The Wasteland."* Under New Criticism 'true German' is simply a statement by the lady that she is not a Russian, but a genuine German.

This book you hold in your hand, however, is something of an autobiography. While New Criticism could be used quite well for my *"1918-20 West Clinch Avenue"* poem, you won't do that. Even though it would work for the poem—the poem is internally consistent, self-referent, it easily stands alone—to read that poem strictly with New Criticism is too ascetic, too narrow. You will not do that because you want to know—and I want you to know—how the train poem fits within the the rest of the boy's autobiography.

You will deduce correctly that this same boy, who earlier built a snow fort in Boston, now knows about death and the possible need for forts. That even though he is only seven, he has father issues. That his electric train enthralls him.

Aside from what you learn about the boy in this book, you as an educated person know that when the boy was seven in 1949, the United States was back-engineering the V2 rocket in Huntsville, with Wernher von Braun on the USA team. That the Saturn V rocket, the Apollo program, and the moon landing would follow fast upon that summer of 1949. That only twenty years later this same little boy would be in Austria and hear by radio 20 July 1969 of the moon landing. But this little boy in 1949 could know nothing of what would come, wholly wrapped up in his train, his cat, and his fast red downhill wagon.

I lived on Clinch Avenue from 1949 to 1952, walking to school every day. Second through fourth grades. You read of that in the poem, *"School, 1949-1952"* above.

Chapter 14

RAY LAMONTAGNE AND DOLLY PARTON

Ray LaMontagne is not going to be all right. He knows where he should be, where the road lies, where the road is he should be walking on, but he's not going to do it.

> *Cocaine playing in my bloodstream,*
> *Sold my coat when I hit Spokane,*
> *Bought myself a hard pack of cigarettes*
> *In the early morning rain.*

He says his hands don't feel like his own, that his eyes are full of dust. He laments the loss of Jolene, whom he held his arms just one time. But he tells her it's too late for him, he's not going to give up the cocaine.

How bad off is he? Pretty bad. He says he woke up face down in a ditch, bloody lips, hair stinking of booze. But he remembers when he had something too good to lose: He has a picture in his pocket of Jolene. He takes it out and looks at it. Says he doesn't know what love means, that he is no longer part of the human race, just living out of a suitcase, traveling, doing drugs.

He knows what to do, where the right road lies: Back to Jolene. But he is not going to do it.

> *Jolene, I ain't about to go straight.*
> *It's too late.*
> *Jolene . . .*
>
> Ray LaMontagne, "Jolene"
Trouble, 2004 Stone Dwarf Records

What to make of this ballad of sadness? Beautiful music, seductive plaintiveness, bewitching in LaMontagne's raspy voice. The sort of thing banned under Mao's Cultural Revolution, or anyone's Cultural Revolution for that matter. It is hopelessly self-indulgent. It is dangerous. It packages cocaine use in a loner anti-hero who makes his way somehow despite deep sadness, despite loss.

Some Sunni Muslims would bulldoze this cultural artifact. Perhaps they should. This version of *"Jolene"* is certainly Exhibit One In Western Decay. Self-indulgent drug-induced navel gazing. Beautiful music.

The other version of *"Jolene,"* Dolly Parton's version, is a militant fight song. Dolly refuses to allow her life to be ruined by a temptress who wants to take her man away. Dolly's words are framed as requests, but the tempo, the energy are strident, rapid, in-your-face.

> *Jolene . . . I'm begging of you please don't take*
> *my man.*
> *Jolene . . . Please don't take him just because*
> *you can.*

Jolene has auburn hair, emerald green eyes, ivory skin, a smile like a breath of spring.

And I cannot compete with you, Jolene.

You have all the advantages, you hussy, but I won't stand for it, you playing those female trump cards.

> *You can have your choice of men*
> *But I could never love again.*
> *He's the only one for me, Jolene.*

So here's how it is, you hussy: You may appear to be in control here, but I am not putting up with it.

> *My happiness depends on you,*
> *And whatever you decide to do, Jolene . . .*
> > Dolly Parton, "Jolene"
> > *1973 RCA Nashville*

No lying face down in the ditch for Dolly. The words speak a request, but Dolly has her claws out. She knows what she has to do, and she is on it. Perhaps she will succeed. She is doing what she can, all that she can. Ray LaMontagne accepts failure, romanticizes it: Woe is me, he says, poor lonely me. Dolly will survive Mao's cultural Revolution. LaMontagne will not.

On a much lighter note, we have Miranda Lambert's reflections upon morality:

> *Oh, me-oh-my-oh,*
> *Would you look at Miss Ohio?*
> *She's riding around with her ragtop down.*
> *Says, "I want to do right, but not right now."*

Situational ethics. She's having fun. She is not alone in her convertible. She's got someone with her. A soldier.

With an arm around her shoulder,
A regimental soldier.
And Mama keeps pushing that wedding gown.

So, Miss Ohio says, maybe there are some nagging questions here, but I am having none of them. I'm having fun.

I know all about it,
So you don't have to shout it.
I'm going to straighten it out somehow.
        —Miranda Lambert, "Look at Miss Ohio"
            Four the Record, 2011 RCA Nashville

She is going to be all right. She is just on a temporary frolic-and-detour. She knows where the road is. Ray LaMontagne does not.

Chapter 15

BOY SCOUTS AND FOOTBALL

This chapter is about the substrate of my political beliefs, about how I somehow became grounded enough to succeed in politics.

Quite simply, the first two cornerstones of my character are Troop Five and high school football. A.B. Wood and B.E. Sharp, respectively. They laid my cornerstones, my scoutmaster and my coach. Formal education did not. A.B. Wood and B.E. Sharp made me capable of politics.

In 1984 in Reno, Nevada, I added the third permanent cornerstone, Christianity.

I can still recite the Boy Scout Law: "A Scout is trustworthy, loyal, helpful, friendly, courteous, kind, obedient, cheerful, thrifty, brave, clean, and reverent." Twelve things to achieve. Quite a job description for age eleven through fourteen.

We sang many songs, still with me. One is particularly poignant, and tough:

> *Have I kept my honor bright?*
> *Can I guiltless sleep tonight?*
> *Have I done and have I dared*
> *Everything to be prepared?*

"Okay," says the sophisticated intellectual, "that song is pap, shallow drivel, mindwash for children." Perhaps so, but I am a sophisticated intellectual. So are you, dear reader, if you have read this far. I do not believe you will brush the song aside as objectionable nonsense, but rather agree with me that simple values simply expressed have a place in the rearing of our children. That we need more Troop Fives.

As I write, I look up to the cubbyholes above my desk. There stand my Eagle Scout ribbon in its presentation box, the Book of Common Prayer, a small American flag, and a ceramic owl given me by a beloved social worker. "You make the world a better place," it says upon the owl's chest. There are also two Teddy bears—the newer one from my daughter. It announced my grandson *in utero*. The older one is mine—worn and patched, re-stuffed and re-fluffed as far as his bare spots will allow.

In Boy Scouts I learned to sharpen an axe, split kindling, make fires, cook over a campfire, use a compass, and tie knots. I learned the structure of city, state, and federal government. I learned First Aid. I learned cooperation and teamwork. I learned exhaustion, and that you can keep going even when exhausted. That was July 1956 in the Order of the Arrow ordeal.

I learned Morse code. I learned the hills of Valley Forge in July of 1957. I learned the backstroke, the breaststroke, and the sidestroke. At Camp Pellissippi I learned I didn't like cold showers, or the smell of pig crap. I learned to love the sound of cicadas and the roar of thunderstorms. I learned that there are assholes in every organization.

I saw the Liberty Bell in Philadelphia and met my Congressman on the steps of the Capitol. I learned to be a useful American, whatever was to come.

In football, I learned that aggression is fun, that it can channeled, and that you can be praised for it. That was novel and delightful. It was like being told, "Hey, it's good to pick your nose. Go for it!" No one before had ever told me to be aggressive.

But my delight in aggression stayed in a compartment, on

the field. I don't know why. I suppose I could have concluded that it was fine to smash people when I was off the field, but I did not make that transference. Though I have a temper, I am largely peaceful. I am not, for example, a participant in road rage; I find it interesting. It is like a deformed beetle, interesting but not attractive.

In football just as in scouting I learned about exhaustion, and that, yes, you can keep going even when exhausted. In football I learned I disliked heat, sweat running in my eyes, and having my finger dislocated. In football I learned more injuries than fingers were out there waiting. I saw a friend's leg broken, a knee dislocated.

I learned there is a rock sticking out of the thirty-five yard line in Coalfield, Tennessee, and that beating Coalfield on their home field means your bus will be vandalized and you'll be late getting back to Knoxville. In football I learned that you can have snot running down your face and that it does not bother you.

Chapter 16

IF THE GERMAN BLUE TICK PICKER HAD MADE IT TO WESTMINSTER

A possible script for the announcer of the Westminster Dog Show:

"The German Blue Tick Picker is a dog with a long and difficult ancestry. From earliest times it has had few friends. Self-possessed, it will not hunt, herd, or retrieve—steadfastly resisting all efforts at utility. The German Blue Tick Picker exists today solely because of his striking devotion to procreation.

Not friendly to children, the Tick Picker requires a great deal of open space for its rambunctious nature. With a matted and twisted coat, the Tick Picker requires daily grooming. This is a dog which gets along best with a servile master.

Despite its name, the German Blue Tick Picker is not picky about food, and will eat almost anything.

The German Blue Tick Picker, number 8."

POLITICS

Chapter 17

POLITICIANS, FRIENDS, AND LAWYERS

If you should consider supporting a politician in an election, what are the character traits you think are absolutely necessary for you to give your endorsement? (Of course, I know that for some people it does not come down to character traits. It comes down to political party.)

In Tennessee politics I am a faithful Republican. In national politics, I am a conservative without a party. But I have many bedfellows inside and outside established political parties. While I care very little for any national political party, I do take character traits most seriously.

I also know that for many people the choice of which politician to support comes down to ending up on the winning side afterwards. Those people try to figure out as best they can who is going to win, and then they support that politician. Period. Winning is everything.

However, people who care a great deal about issues pick the politician who has a significant chance of winning, and also most closely agrees with them. The congruence need not be perfect. Close is good enough. If that's the best there is, they will hold their noses and cast a vote for a (flawed) standard bearer. They will not support a candidate who is perfect on the issues, but who also has no chance of prevailing. For them a "protest" vote is silliness, a wasted vote.

Politicians

So: character traits. Which ones are indispensable to you in a politician? Let's be careful here, for it is easy to trot out high-sounding platitudes.

I personally would start by requiring that my politician be true to his/her core beliefs. The one-word platitude for that is *integrity*. I do not have to share those core beliefs. They do not have to be my core beliefs. Ronald Reagan and Jimmy Carter were fine men of equal integrity. I never voted for Carter, but I always admired him.

Obviously, what set those two men apart in the hard world of elected politics was policy. Some of those policy differences sprang from their differences in core beliefs. But they never waffled on their core beliefs. They never were—as so often happens nowadays—"for" something before being later "against it."

The politician of my heart must also be *moral*; he must do no harm to his fellow citizens. He must be *kind*. His morality need not be a specifically articulated Christian morality, but it must be an articulated code of social conduct which respects and honors all persons in his society.

My politician must be *honest* in all things, great and small. He must never steal, never cheat, and when speaking, speak only the truth. It need not be the whole truth, but what is uttered must stand up.

He must be *loyal* to his friends and to his country.

He must *not be narcissistic*, because that impairs vision.

He must be *hardworking* and *sober*.

He must be *organized*, or nothing will get done.

And that's it. A short list, but an idealistic one. In sum:

1. *Not a narcissist*
2. *Integrity (true to his core beliefs)*
3. *Morality*
4. *Kindness to fellow citizens,*
5. *Honesty in all things spoken*
6. *Loyal to his friends and country*
7. *Hardworking*
8. *Sober*
9. *Organized*

(Obviously, there are successful politicians who do not have all these traits. I avoid those politicians.) Is this list too much to ask? No. The difficulty comes when we seek a politician who has these characteristics and also the policies we support.

Say, for example, that you support limited government, a balanced budget, and strong national defense. To get the policies, you may have to reduce your list of character traits. Or, if character traits are your pole star, you may have to choke on some policy shortcomings.

It is interesting that my ideal politician need not be likable, courteous, well educated, or speak good English. Of course, he probably will have some of those qualities, but he need not. For me at least.

Friends

Let us change gears now and ask: What are the character traits you find necessary in a friend? Some are probably the same ones you found you needed in your ideal politician. Obviously, your friend *cannot be a narcissist.* (A narcissist has only one friend, himself.) But, in my opinion, he must have *integrity, honesty, kindness,* and *loyalty.* What needs to be added? Well, I think your ideal friend must *share a number of interests* with you. And maybe that is it. A pretty short list. In sum:

1. *Not a narcissist*
2. *Integrity (true to his core beliefs)*
3. *Honesty in all things spoken*
4. *Kindness*
5. *Loyalty to you*
6. *Shared interests*

It is interesting to me is that—while I would prefer it—my friend need not be moral, sober, organized, speak good English, or work hard. He probably will have some of these desirable qualities, but he need not. Which leads me to imagine myself marooned on a desert island with my immoral, drunk, disorganized, lazy friend who murders the King's English. I hope I get rescued soon.

Lawyers

Let's now turn one more corner and ask what traits are necessary for your ideal lawyer. (I have a lawyer friend who says it is important to avoid lawyers who advertise on TV. That may mean you won't find a lawyer today.)

Clearly, your lawyer *cannot be a narcissist*. He or she must have *integrity*, and be of *good morals*. He must be *kind, likable, loyal to you, courteous,* and *sober*. He must speak and write *excellent English* in order to practice law effectively. He must be *hardworking, honest,* and *organized*. Rather a long list. In sum:

1. *Not a narcissist*
2. *Integrity (true to his core beliefs)*
3. *Morality*
4. *Kind*
5. *Likable*
6. *Loyal to you*
7. *Courteous*
8. *Sober*

9. *Speaks and writes excellent English*
10. *Hardworking*
11. *Honesty in all things spoken*
12. *Organized*

So, looking at the three lists of qualities needed in politicians, friends, and attorneys, the analysis, if accurate, means that we may have or should have higher standards for our lawyers than for our friends or politicians.

The White Lie

All three—politician, friend, and lawyer—are allowed to tell white lies. White lies are permissible distortions done for moral reasons:

- *"Belgium is a valuable ally."*
- *"No, you do not look fat in that dress."*
- *"I have been thinking about your case a lot lately."*

A white lie is not a self-deception. It is a benign deception practiced upon others for what we think are good reasons. But to say, "Everyone else is doing it," is not a white lie. That is a self-directed absolution in which you tell yourself, "Well, I may be a little less than pure here, but, don't you see, I am in good company? It must be all right."

The same goes for that great phrase, "I paid for it." This is not a white lie. This comes from what your mother may have told you once, "It's OK, darlin', you paid for it. Just take the motel towel."

Really? If it's OK to take the motel towel, is it OK to take the motel's lamps and pictures as well? Is it just a problem of a slippery slope? Is morality really only a question of degree?

Chapter 18

THE 1982 JUDICIAL CAMPAIGN

I want to give you an insider's look at my four judicial campaigns.

In some states, judicial terms last four, or six, or even fourteen years. But in Tennessee and many other states, a full judicial term lasts eight years. I am going to give you some details for the campaigns of 1982, 1990, 1998, and 2006.

For the 1982 campaign, my father was my main contributor. It was for an open judgeship. If my fine Republican predecessor, George Child, had not filled out his full eight-year term, the Democrat governor would have appointed a successor. Judge Child did not want that to happen.

I had an excellent campaign manager, Joe May. A campaign for a completely open seat, no incumbent, can be a free-for-all. With my father's support and Joe's guidance, I pulled it off. After my re-election in August 1990, my father died in October from an abdominal aortic aneurysm, the same thing which killed his own father. I've got three of those "triple A's." Life is precious.

The particular mortality of my male forebears weighs on me, yes, but pleasantly. I do not worry. I know that life is precious and that I am blessed to have additional years of life.

In October of 2014 I did have an aortic event—but not where it was "supposed" to be, in the abdomen. I decided to impress everybody, go right to the top, the top of the aortic tree, the ascending aorta. I now have four inches of new aorta coming from my heart. My favorite cloth in the whole wide world is dacron.

1982 was rough-and-tumble, an education. Fully as rich and intricate as my Yale doctoral experience. I campaigned door-to-door but—thanks to Joe—only in those parts of the city and county known to turn out for Republican primaries. The faithful.

I cut through yards to save time. I got bitten twice by dogs, got a tan, and lost ten pounds. If no one answered the door, I put a campaign card on the door, writing on it, "Sorry I missed you, Bill." That and direct mailings were what won the primary.

Here is one piece from the direct mail campaign:

> *Dear Neighbor:*
>
> *In the upcoming May 4th election, you will make a decision which will affect many people. The race I'm talking about is for Judge of the Fourth Circuit Court, the Domestic Relations Court. Because the importance of this position is often overlooked, I felt I needed to talk with you.*
>
> *I have never written a letter like this before, but I believe the stakes are great in this election. In the Republican Primary there are four candidates, and I know them all to be conscientious and qualified. But one stands out. That's Bill Swann.*
>
> *As a lawyer, Bill has an impeccable reputation. Not only is he extremely proficient in his knowledge of the law, but he is also genuinely interested in people. This, I believe, is what will make Bill Swann a great judge.*
>
> *It is not an easy job. But Bill has the judicial temperament and patience to deal with domestic cases in a fair and impartial manner.*
>
> *There are many things I could say about Bill Swann, but let me simply say that one of Bill's most*

important qualities is that he cares about family life and values.

I hope you will make your decision carefully in the upcoming election, and join me in voting for Bill Swann on May 4ᵗʰ in the Republican Primary.
Sincerely,
L. Anderson Galyon III

One of the doors I went to produced a fine elderly couple who were most interested in what I had to say. Remembering Joe's counsel not to spend overly long at a location, I wound up the conversation asking if I could count on them in the upcoming primary. They said no, they didn't think so. I said I was sorry, and might I ask why? Well, they said, because their son Bob Godwin was running against me.

The May 1982 primary was just the beginning, the Master's Degree in elected office politics, if you will. I only had to win the primary by a plurality of the votes cast for the four contenders. And that's how it turned out:

- Swann   7,228 (37.9%)
- Bob Godwin   4,692 (24.6%)
- Marty McDonald   4,267 (22.4%)
- Jim Pryor   2,871 (15.1%)

The Ph.D. in elected office politics came in the general election of August 1982. I faced Democrat Frankie Wade who herself had won a hard primary, a three-way. We were two experienced campaigners at this point, going head-to-head. The great unknown was how would voters respond to a female candidate?

There were few women lawyers in Tennessee in 1982 and almost no female judges. My opponent was heavily financed by her husband, a medical doctor and the brother of Gary Wade, our supreme court justice. All turned out well for me in the election after a few more dogs, lots of direct mail, and countless Rotary, Kiwanis, and Optimist luncheons:

- Swann   24,778 (56.9%);
- Wade   18,733 (43.1%)

Choosing judges by partisan election is bad. Sometimes just having an R or D after your name is all that is necessary. In my judicial district in 2014 that was the case.

Choosing judges by nonpartisan election is bad. Generally, there is so little interest in judicial elections that a large quantity of money can get any bozo elected. That's bad enough. But to make things worse, money has strings on it. I had one fellow attempt to call in his chips soon after I was on the bench in 1982. I looked up his donation ($500), mailed him a $500 check, and recused myself from his litigation. No, I am not purer than driven snow, but I got that one right.

Choosing judges by gubernatorial appointment is bad. A governor has favors to return. Appointing judges is one of those favors a governor can do. Those favors may be consonant with appointee excellence or not. Even if so-called "blue ribbon" panels propose names to the governor, those panels are heavily interest-oriented The panels recommend names accordingly.

Choosing judges by any method yet devised is bad. So name your poison. Judgeships are alarmingly powerful and invasive. The person on the bench can be narrow and arrogant.

In my strong opinion, judgeships must not be filled by lazy lawyers, persons seeking sinecures, political appointees, or self-important individuals. There's an old saying, "If you want to find the S.O.B. in a man, put a black robe on him."

A lazy judge is a blight on the community, a betrayal of the disadvantaged, a hindrance to the bar, a disgrace to the law. And he will be unchecked, as there are no internal mechanisms to promote efficient case management, orderly docket flow, or even to see that at least forty hours are spent on the job. It comes down to individual devotion-to-task. Some judges lack that.

Chapter 19

THE 1990 JUDICIAL CAMPAIGN

My 1990 re-election was a cake walk. There was no opposition in either party.

The Sixth Judicial District of Tennessee is heavily Republican, so you attend all twelve Republican club meetings throughout the district, at least four every month, ideally throughout your eight-year term of office. But definitely in the year before an election.

That is supposed to assure that you do not have Republican opposition. You are the speaker at some club meetings, you lead the pledge at some, and you shake-and-howdy at all of them. A wag said it's like kissing your sister: You have to do it, but there's not much in it for you. Still it was necessary to prepare for the possibility of a contest:

- *file a qualification petition*
- *appoint a treasurer*
- *do direct mailings to the bar*
- *raise funds*
- *meet all qualification deadlines*
- *prepare direct mail pieces for use when and if opposition appears*
- *disclose funds raised and expended, and*
- *speak, speak, speak at public gatherings.*

8 February 1990 the following appeared in the Knoxville *Journal*:

Swann to run for re-election as circuit judge

Fourth Circuit Judge William K. Swann announced Wednesday he will seek re-election to a second term.

Swann, 47, will be a candidate for the Republican nomination in the May 1 county-wide primary.

"My first term as a circuit court judge has been challenging and satisfying. There are few opportunities for community service as direct as a judgeship," Swann said.

Swann, who was first elected in 1982, is a member of the Knox County Task Force against Domestic Violence. He also served as a faculty adviser to the National Judicial College and serves on the executive committee of the Tennessee Judicial Conference.

He is a graduate of the University of Tennessee College of Law and is a member of the Knoxville, Tennessee, and American bar associations.

Swann has been voted Man of the Year by both the Knoxville Area Social Workers and the Tennessee Young Lawyers Conference.

The most delightful letter of support I received came from Phil Durand, with the firm of Ambrose, Wilson, Grimm & Durand. Phil was a lawyer to whom I had sent a solicitation in a direct mail attorney mail-out:

November 22, 1989

Right Honorable Bwana Swann, Sir:

You have my support!! You also asked for my advice. No judge I have ever known or appeared before has ever paid the slightest bit of attention to my advice. Don't disgrace the judiciary by letting the illusion get about that you would pay any attention to my advice even were I to offer it.

Instead I have prepared an election campaign poster which emphasizes your venerable decades of service to all and sundry. (All died recently, and Sundry is the lady you threw out on the street after 28 years of marriage with naught but $28 of rehabilitative alimony to help her find a new job at age 48.)

> *Re-elect Bill Swann Judge: After all, where else can you find years and years and years of accumulated wisdom and experience, all of which can be expressed in opinions written in flawless German? Contempt of Court is punishable by a wrong-way trip through the Berlin Wall and tea with Egon Krenz.*

I think I spotted you on top of the Berlin Wall with the students in the Time Magazine picture, but I won't mention it to the press if you refrain from throwing me in jail for contempt of court for writing this letter.

In addition to levity there were heartwarming, serious letters. One of the dearest came from Fred Musick, a past president of the Knoxville Bar Association, a man with whom I had crossed swords as an attorney:

November 20, 1989
Dear Bill,
Thank you so much for your letter to me of
November 15, 1989.
I will certainly be pleased to support you in your
bid for re-election. You do have a difficult position
to fill, and in my opinion, you have well done so.
. . .
Incidentally, as you know, I had hoped that you
would be appointed as one of our Federal Judges
[He had nominated me.] but the political situation
apparently required someone from the First District
to be appointed, rather than from our District.
With all best wishes and kind personal regards . . .

That federal nomination got off to a rocky start. When the
Justice Department called to interview the managing partner of
Hogin, Guyton, Swann & London, my partner John Hogin just
knew it was Courtney Pearre who often called in with an assumed
identity:

"Mr. Hogin, the Justice Department is on line two."
"Thank you, Mary."
John punched line two on the intercom: *"Don't worry,"* John
said, *"I'm sending the cocaine back."*
"Excuse me? Is this Mr. John Hogin, the senior partner?
This is Robert Smith of the Justice Department. I'm calling from
Washington."
"Oh, well, you see, Mr. Smith, it's like this . . ."

In the 1990 election a four-page, 11"x14" single-spaced hate
piece appeared. You may recall that I said the 1982 campaign
was "rough and tumble," an educational foray fully as rich and
intricate as the Yale graduate school experience. 1990 deepened

the richness. Let me share some typical nuggets, should any readers be contemplating entering politics:

Dear Democrat and Independent voter:

NOW IS THE TIME TO UNITE and get rid of the most corrupt, incompetent gang of crooks and rogues who ever banded together to take over a County Government. The Republicans holding office now in Knox County are absolutely the worst public officials in the history of Knox County. We can beat them all if we get organized and work hard. But we have to tell the truth on them and stay united. We need to fill out our Democrat Ticket by nominating some good Democrats by using the write-in vote in races where we do not now have a candidate.

In what follows in this piece, I insert initials instead of the real names of the real people who were named. I do not correct spelling, grammar, or punctuation:

*First there is ignorant, drunk and crooked **A**, Republican [incumbent of office **B**]. He will be easy beat. A was arrested for drunk driving and beat the case by "buying off" the District Attorney General, bringing in a crooked special Judge from Roane County to "fix" his case and got two crooked Judges from Knox County to commit perjury and swear he was not drunk when he left the Bistro Bar in downtown Knoxville. The two crooked judges who were witnesses for **A** were **C** and **D** . . . **A** is one of the biggest drunks in Knox County, a whore monger and drug and cocaine user. He is never in*

*his office and does not do any work . . . except walk
the halls of City-County Building and gossip . . .*

*The Republicans are getting ready to nominate a
well known whore for [office E]; that is a woman
named F. . . . This bitch has shacked up for years
with a Jew named G . . . and has tried to separate
him from his wife . . .*

*Without doubt the worst and crookedest [holder of
office H] is J. The Criminal Court of Appeals and
the Supreme Court of Tennessee have said he is
incompetent and ineffective as a lawyer . . . J is well
known in Drug and Cocaine circles of Knoxville
as a Cocaine addict. He has a large number of
crooked defense lawyers as friends and they funnell
Cocaine, Marihuana and cash to him and he just
fixes their client's cases by refusing to prosecute
their cases. The leaders of the crooked lawyers are
K, L, M (a Cocaine addict himself), N . . .*

*That fellow, O, from South Knoxville, is the son of
old Preacher P, the crooked radio preacher, who
was involved in a big Sequoyah scandal 30 years
ago involving the severe molestation of a baby boy
by O's other son. He almost chewed off the little
boys penis. The P family are all queers. O [holder of
office Q], is also a queer and now lives with another
male queer in South Knoxville. O is well known
in Knoxville's Gay (queer) community as a queer
and many reputable people have seen him in the
company of known queers . . .*

R in Fountain City is one of the biggest whores ever known in Knox County . . . R and S are opposed to most qualified candidates unless they are whores, lesbian queers or male queers. We need to write-in a qualified candidate against R in the May 1 Primary.

I apologize for the length of the foregoing. I know it is unpleasant. I wanted you to have a bellyful of the crazed cant that inhabits the periphery of elected office. This language of hate is not unique to 1990, nor unique to any electoral district. There are bad people out there, and some of them want to hurt you. This sort of language reappeared sixteen years later in my 2006 campaign.

Chapter 20

THE 1998 JUDICIAL CAMPAIGN

Eight years earlier I had had no opposition in either party. In 1998 it turned out to be slightly different: There was sham opposition in the Republican party primary. That is, for a while.

An attorney who practiced before me, Tom Monceret, took out a petition to run with the Knox County Election Commission. Then after a number of weeks he withdrew his petition, having accomplished some newspaper notice and—as he put it to me later—"jerking me around for a while." Such are the joys of politics.

Several things accounted for the lack of real opposition. One was the daunting fact that my elected position, Fourth Circuit Court, was firmly on its way to becoming the busiest court of record in the state. That made it a job not many lawyers wanted. But the second reason for no real attorney opposition in 1998 was that the Fourth Circuit was an efficient, organized court most domestic lawyers wanted to use.

I introduced conferences to Knox County for pretrial management. They quickly became a popular feature of the court's docket. It was an innovation, yes, but not brain surgery. Just common sense. However, it overturned decades of ingrained attorney habit—habit which most of the time had led to disorganized, rambling trials which cost clients dearly and—from my perspective as administrator—cost the court calendar even more dearly.

There were other innovations which were noticed and appreciated, pretty much "inside baseball" details I will not dwell on.

A third reason for no 1998 opposition was editorial notice that Fourth Circuit dealt with unpleasant problems, and did it pretty well. In December of 1995 Janet Tate wrote a long piece called "Judgment Days" for *Metropulse*, our local weekly, which set the stage of a typical courtroom showdown:

> *It's Wednesday morning in Fourth Circuit Court, and as on every other Wednesday (and Monday, and Tuesday) a divorce trial is in session. Outside, the day dawns slow and windy; inside Judge Bill Swann's clean, well-lighted courtroom in the City-County building downtown, the matter of* Smith vs. Smith *(not their real names) is back on the docket.*
>
> *Like the 200 or so other contested divorce actions heard in this court alone every year, the issues in the* Smith *case never seem to die, or even fade away very much; this particular human drama has been on and off the court's schedule for more than four years now.*
>
> *Today the ex-Mrs. Smith's attorney is grilling Mr. Smith about the post-judgment sale of some personal property. Mr. Smith, who bears a passing resemblance to the dweebish brother Niles on the TV sitcom Frazier—alternately squirms, shuffles through sheaves of papers, and glares from the witness stand. His ex-wife hugs herself protectively and sits, tight-lipped and motionless.*

Then Janet Tate moved on to a bit of reflection:

> *When you hear about the raw deal your brother or your best friend got in divorce court, consider this: A judge hearing a bitterly-contested divorce case has the impossible job of within a few hours disentangling people's lives and trying to make them happy when they are at their angriest and most hurt, living through what is likely to be the most devastating period of their lives.*

As I say, the public's perception of the court, and more importantly, the lawyers' perception of the court, was that it was a tough job.

A fourth reason for no opposition in 1998 was wholly unexpected. In 1979 the legislature had passed a civil statute on domestic abuse—orders of protection—which was a sleeper. It provided civil remedies for domestic abuse but in the beginning no one used it. Attorneys deemed it an unnecessary alternative to criminal prosecutions, or to prohibitive injunctions available in circuit or chancery court.

The first civil orders of protection were brought in Fourth Circuit Court six years after passage of the statute. In 1985 ten cases were docketed—cases which I agreed to entertain as an experiment at the request of one attorney, Jean Munroe. Those ten cases were followed in 1986 by hundreds of cases, and then thousands in the years leading up to 1998. Again Janet Tate, December 1995:

> *Thursday in Fourth Circuit Court is reserved as order of protection day, and the week after Thanksgiving there's a packed house in Swann's courtroom.*

Even so, the room is eerily silent, save for the occasional whimper of a young child.

No one in this crowded room wants to be here, not the red-eyed women huddled near the back and perimeters of the room, not the sullen-faced men who mostly sit hunched or sprawl-legged toward the front or slouch against the walls, hands jammed deep into jacket pockets . . .

A table in front of the judge's bench bears neatly stacked handouts, explaining the legal definitions and ramifications of such topics as substance abuse, stalking, and telephone problems.

I had unwittingly, naively, compounded my docket overload by making a "deal" with the three judges in Chancery Court: They would take all the adoption filings under a newly revised statute on that topic, and I would take all the order of protection filings under the new O/P statute. This is the sort of bargain Jack made, trading his mother's cow for magic beans. The beanstalk that grew for me did not rise to a magic land with a harp and a golden goose.

Presently a slide show starts. Judge Swann takes up his microphone and, acting as a sort of master of ceremonies, begins explaining the vagaries of courtroom protocol and case preparation to the standing-room-only crowd.

At times Swann's voice rises with the timbre and cadence of, if not an evangelist, then perhaps an Episcopalian priest, as he delivers a message to the masses that is part law, part psychology, part no-nonsense law enforcement.

He explains the concept of "preponderance of evidence" as it applies to violence and destruction of property.

He admits to flaws in the system, and apologizes for them. He points out that he doesn't make the law, he just applies it. And he makes it clear to those in attendance that . . . orders of protection will be obeyed, with sobering consequences for those who choose to ignore them.

Filings for civil orders of protection continued to rise after the 1998 election, making this judgeship even less attractive to lawyers looking for something to do other than private practice. But that did not prevent a bitter contested election contest in 2006.

Chapter 21

2001 WAS NOT A GOOD YEAR

But before the 2006 campaign there was the momentous year 2001. It was not a good year for the United States, nor at times for me. When the second plane hit the World Trade Center, I went to our front porch and put up our American flag. It has flown there without interruption ever since.

What was I doing? Symbolic resistance, yes. I wanted to escape the horrid feelings of being alone, isolated, vulnerable. All irrational feelings of course: I was no more alone on nine-eleven than I had been on nine-ten, but I felt alone. I came in from the porch and went to Diana. We held each other.

And, just weeks before nine-eleven, *"Judge Has Brain Surgery,"* the newspaper had screamed. Always great for the 2006 re-election campaign. Always great for courthouse rumors.

Two months before nine-eleven, I discovered I had a pituitary adenoma, a benign tumor crushing the pituitary gland. I discovered it only when there was a rupture with amazing pain. Galloping nausea. I tried to vomit up my small and large intestines.

Diana drove me to the emergency room at UT Hospital. And— wouldn't you know it?—the rupture was missed by the emergency room CT scan. (No, I did not sue.)

After thirteen hours wasted in the emergency room, the following colorful set-to with the attending incompetent E.R.

physician occurred. (I later learned he was not an M.D., but rather an O.D., doctor of osteopathy). Did his degree make a difference? Probably not. Incompetence is incompetence no matter the degree it wears.

> *"You have a migraine."*
> *"No, doctor, I do not. I have never had a migraine in my life. My wife has migraines. I know migraines."*
> *(This with my eyes screwed shut and tears running down my cheeks.)*
> *"You've been vomiting."*
> *"Look, I know vomiting can be a symptom of migraines. This is not a migraine. It's something else. I can't open my eyes. The light hurts."*
> *"Photophobic," the doctor said.*
> *"Yeah. I know the Greek. This is not a migraine."*

"Now Mr. Swann, migraines can be strange. Adult onset is possible. It's in the literature. We've done a CT scan. I see no evidence of bleeding or tumor in your brain. What would you have us do now?"

> *"You told me I have blood in the spinal fluid."*
> *"Yes. The spinal tap itself can cause that. It must have been a traumatic stick, a dirty stick. I'm sure of it."*
> *I heard him writing on the chart. "I'm sending you home with two prescriptions. Imitrex for the pain, and Phenergan suppositories for nausea."*
> *"Doctor, this is not a migraine. Don't send me home."*
> *"Mr. Swann, it is. I am the doctor. Have your wife take you home now."*
> *"Doctor . . ."*
> *"Goodbye, Mr. Swann."*

Twenty hours later, I was back. This time, I bypassed the fool in the emergency room, got admitted directly to the hospital by John Dougherty, a neurologist friend. My electrolytes could barely be measured. The fool in the E.R. had nearly killed me.

It was "just" a pituitary tumor. It had ruptured, causing acute symptoms. Simple. A completely benign tumor. A physical presence. No problem if diagnosed and removed promptly. The CT ordered by the incompetent O.D. had actually suggested its presence—the blood in the spinal fluid was caused by the rupture of the tumor. An MRI found it immediately upon the hospital admission.

The mistake by the O.D. was not ordering the CT to go down far enough to include the pituitary sella. If you don't ask for the inclusion, you don't get it. If you do ask for it, you won't need the MRI. The tumor will be obvious on the CT. And you don't get sent home, with wrong and dangerous prescriptions.

But all turned out well. As I said, I did not sue. There's enough of that going around. The tumor's remains were removed. Walgreens entered my life, my new buddy, a zillion prescriptions for daily complete hormone replacement therapy. Me and Barry Bonds shooting up in the men's room.

My endocrinologist tells me only seven-tenths of one percent of all pituitary adenomas result in apoplexy, the sudden dramatic crisis. She also tells me that most of her patients just give up after a pituitary adenoma: "They let themselves go. They don't try any more." "Why?" I asked, "It's so easy to manage hormone replacement." "I don't know," she said, "I guess it's just such a setback."

Chapter 22

THE 2006 JUDICIAL CAMPAIGN

In 2006 the outpouring of support for me from the local bar was overwhelming, heartwarming, and most welcome. I suspect it was as much for me as it was against my opponent, David Lee, but I do not know.

One hundred and twenty lawyers comprised the letterhead of the Bill Swann Campaign Committee. 21 December 2005 two of them wrote to their fellow lawyers on the letterhead of the campaign:

> *Dear Colleague,*
> *We know how important Judge Bill Swann is to the Knoxville Bar Association and the people of Knox County. We practice in his court. . . .*
> *In civil courts of record, Judge Swann's caseload is unmatched across the state of Tennessee. Indeed, it is not even approached. In the last fiscal year for which there are figures, he disposed of over four thousand (4,000) cases.*
> *He is a nationally recognized, widely published, speaker on family law. He teaches at the National Judicial College and the Tennessee Judicial Conference. Additionally, he trains all*

new Tennessee judges after their election or appointment . . .

Campaigns are expensive. Please make your check to the Bill Swann Campaign Committee, and mail it to Jim London, Treasurer, in the enclosed envelope . . .

Sincerely,

Elizabeth K.B. Meadows

Jerrold L. Becker

One of the most effective late pieces sent to the bar was a 12 April 2006 letter by four attorneys—Sam English, Jim London, and the same Jerry Becker and Betsy Meadows above. The point was ignorance is not bliss:

Dear Colleague:

It appears there will not be a Knoxville Bar Association poll conducted on the qualifications of the two candidates for Fourth Circuit Court. This means that a serious mistake could happen. It also means that you are very important in the next few weeks.

Judge Swann's opponent is running an expensive campaign to unseat him. He has a campaign headquarters on Kingston Pike; he has a traveling Ad-Mobile truck; he is spending money to get to the voters.

The voters won't know the difference between these two candidates unless we tell them.

That's why the four of us are writing you. We want you to commit to talking to your friends and family about Judge Swann between now and May 2.

Tell them, tell your clients, how strongly you feel about the choice. Tell them:

—that Judge Swann has the respect of his peers, both lawyers and judges;

—that he works tirelessly as a judge;

—that he teaches all newly elected Tennessee judges before they go on the bench, and recently taught evidence to all circuit and appellate judges of Tennessee;

—that the <u>only</u> qualified candidate for Fourth Circuit is Judge Bill Swann.

This race is too important to leave to chance. Early voting starts April 12, and the election itself is May 2 . . .

The reason there was no 2006 bar poll of lawyers on the suitability of a candidate or incumbent for a judgeship (first sentence in the letter above) was federal district court judge Jimmy Jarvis. His wife Gail, who in the previous election cycle had been a sitting general sessions court judge, was savaged in that year's bar poll. She was then defeated. He attacked the Knoxville Bar Association for running such a poll.

Early voting had become an increasingly important factor in 2006. At various times in April the following was published, carrying the names of sixty-four attorneys:

An Open Letter to the Voters of Knox County

We are lawyers who practice in the Knox County Fourth Circuit Court.

We have represented you, your loved ones, and friends in all of the issues that come into that court . . .

We cannot allow this judgeship to be used as a target for one person's anger.

*We are deeply concerned that you may vote on the
basis of a few distorted statements containing half-
truths, and outright falsehoods . . .*

*A person who has publicly written that he would
resign if elected is not a qualified candidate for this
position . . .*

Not all lawyers supported me, however. 29 April 2006, three
days before the May 2 election, the following appeared as a letter
to the editor in our only daily newspaper:

David Lee would make a good circuit judge

*This is to advise that I have been a member of the
Knoxville Bar for some 49 years and have been in
active practice in this community for all those years
except for the three years that I served in the U.S.
Army as a judge advocate general officer.*

*Throughout the course of the last year, I have
gotten to know David Lee as adversary counsel,
co-counsel, and as a colleague. Although frequent
comments are made concerning Lee, I have found
him to be well educated, competent, responsible,
and always prepared.*

*He has demonstrated legal acumen in the cases
in which I have been involved with him and, as
an adversary, strikes a keen balance between
assertiveness and appropriate reserve. I have seen
nothing that would demonstrate anything other
than he would have a fine judicial temperament
as a judge.*

Lee is from a family of outstanding attorneys and would serve this county very well as its 4th Circuit judge.

—John D. Lockridge Jr.
Knoxville

That letter was placed in the *News Sentinel* probably in response to what had been published 24 April by my campaign. The piece was rendered on letterhead stationery of "Robin S. Kuykendall, Counsel, Advocate & Attorney at Law":

Dear Knox County Voters:

I am a rarity, one of a tiny group of people in Judge Swann's courtroom last year when David Lee, now candidate for Judge Swann's seat, left himself no alternative but the jailhouse for refusing to support his own child. I coincidentally waited there for another matter, which meant I saw and heard the whole hearing on Lee v. Lee.

On the mother's side, Knoxville attorney Wanda Sobieski cross-examined Mr. Lee. Mr. Lee represented himself.

From the mother, a lady from a foreign nation who now struggles to re-educate and support herself and her child, we learned that Mr. Lee had not complied with his duty to support his child.

From Mr. Lee, we learned that, yes, he had not made his payments for quite a while. However, Mr. Lee lamented that he had been unable to help his child because of all the money he lost in business.

Law practice, a risky business, to be sure? No. Mr. Lee had spent hundreds of thousands of dollars examining, flying, and purchasing airplanes while his child went without. He so much as admitted that he spent very little time actually working in his prepared profession.

It was apparent from the proceedings that the parties had been before Judge Swann several times before that, over the same problem. Mr. Lee had never mended his ways, though given many opportunities.

Ms. Sobieski, usually surgical and relentless in the courtroom, showed some of the most respectful deference to an opponent that I have ever seen. Judge Swann showed the same respect throughout.

For the professionals in the room, the issue was not who would mete the sentence or who would receive it. The issue was the integrity of the court and the authority of its orders. The facts were inescapable, and the child support order was the order ignored. If the order was burdensome, Mr. Lee had never done what was necessary to prove it and get the order changed. As a lawyer, he knew the procedure.

Mr. Lee left no choice for the court, no matter who might have been sitting on the bench that day. It would be a difficult situation for any Knox County judge to send a member of the Knox County attorneys' bar to the Knox County Jail for contempt of court.

I don't know how it could have been handled any more carefully or judiciously than was the case of the deadbeat, David Lee. If that's what it took to get David Lee to pay his child support and keep his intelligent, well-spoken, former wife off of the public rolls for even a few months, then Judge Swann can be credited.

I would like to know on election day how much David Lee spent on his campaign, and compare that figure to how much he has paid toward the support and development of his child. Let's hope the latter is the larger, and that Mr. Lee's business ventures are capable of supporting both, as well.

I have to say that I do not agree with all the decisions Judge Swann has made in cases I have brought before him, but that is not the point, anyway. The law, and the courts that enforce it, must be no respecter of persons if any of us are to rely on the law for fairness in our lives.

I may disagree with Judge Swann sometimes, but I do rest assured that both of us hold the law in the highest respect.

Just as the facts of David Lee's child support problem left the court with no alternative but to enforce the law of the State of Tennessee, the facts of the personal vindictiveness of David Lee's attempt to unseat the judge who sent him to jail leave me with no choice but to air my eyewitness testimony now.

David Lee had his day in court and lost, but he apparently never got over it. His actions show us that he is a "respecter of persons" not a respecter of the law. He should never be entrusted with the futures of the thousands of Knox County children whose lives are impacted every day by the orders of Knox County Circuit Court, Division IV.

On 28 April, four days later, seventy-four lawyers published the following paid advertising in the *News Sentinel*:

The JUDGE who will serve for the next 8 years as Judge for the Fourth Circuit Court . . . will be determined in the REPUBLICAN PRIMARY on MAY 2, 2006, <u>not</u> THE GENERAL ELECTION . . . We, the attorneys listed below, collectively have appeared before Judge Swann in literally thousands of cases. We respect his work and have confidence in the service he has provided . . . David Lee, Judge Swann's opponent in this primary, has had only 11 cases in Fourth Circuit Court . . .

The attorney support dearest to me, however, came from the friend I had defeated in 1982. 28 April 2006, the same day as the above, Bob Godwin's letter to the editor was published in the *News Sentinel*:

I have known Bill Swann since 1957. I have been friends with Bill Swann since 1957.
I ran against him in 1982 in the primary and, on coming in second, threw my sincere and enthusiastic support to him in his successful campaign for the judgeship.

I have appeared in 4ᵗʰ Circuit Court thousands of times since returning from the U.S. Army in 1968, many of those before Swann. I respect his integrity, impartiality, fairness and patience.

I have never seen David Lee in 4ᵗʰ Circuit Court except as a party in his own acrimonious divorce.

I continue to support Swann without any reservation whatsoever and urge others to do so in the Republican primary where the race will be decided, as there is no Democrat opposition.

Perhaps the best way to give you a flavor of the campaign is simply to set out some of the ways reporters played it in the press. David Lee and I sold a lot of newspapers for the Knoxville *News Sentinel*. 29 April 2006 a columnist wrote:

The campaign for the Circuit Court judgeship that handles domestic relations escalated this week when incumbent Judge Bill Swann mailed a brochure criticizing opponent David Lee's contributions to Democrats . . .

Swann cites records from the Federal Election Commission on Lee's contributions to a number of Democratic candidates . . . "With these contributions, it is dishonest to call yourself a 'true conservative,'" Swann said in a statement.

That April 29 piece appeared eight days after I had received the endorsement of the *News Sentinel*. That endorsement had come 21 April 2006, just eleven days before the Republican primary:

EDITORIAL
Swann for circuit judgeship;
Jarvis for clerk

The contest for judgeship of the Circuit Court, Division IV, might be one of the most acrimonious races in the Knox County primary. It pits a longtime incumbent against someone who practiced in his court, was temporarily barred from it and believes it is time for a change.

The incumbent is Judge Bill Swann, and the challenger is David Lee . . .

Swann has been on the bench since 1982, and he has done much more than merely decide cases. He is a founding member of the Community Coalition on Family Violence, which works to foster a trusting relationship between the court and its partner agencies. He has worked with Knoxville Mayor Bill Haslam and Knox County Mayor Mike Ragsdale to establish the Family Justice Center, which is expected to open next month and will include 63 partner agencies.

He has established an admirable working relationship with the University of Tennessee, his law school alma mater. Those include "docket days," when the Fourth Circuit Court each October holds its entire docket at the law school as part of Domestic Violence Awareness Month.

The UT College of Nursing and the Roane State Community College nursing classes also attend the Circuit Court sessions. Swann also has initiated the use of clinical psychologists as court witnesses in contested custody cases and initiated standard co-parenting schedules.

Much about this contest is personal, at least from the challenge offered by Lee, who was jailed for a time by Swann on a charge of civil contempt.

Lee argues that term limits apply to judges . . . Lee invoked the term limits argument and added: "If elected the undersigned will immediately resign. Thus, the campaign is only about whether Bill Swann should be retained."

Lee might be an effective judge, but it is difficult to determine that in this campaign.

Perhaps more than in other courts, this one needs a judge with patience, guidance, perseverance, compassion—and a thick hide. Swann has demonstrated these characteristics and deserves another term on the bench.

This endorsement was critical, and not easily won. In the week prior I had learned that the paper—which leans heavily to Democrat party candidates and Democrat issues—was preparing to endorse Lee. Which figured, given the stature of Lee's father, J.D. Lee, in Tennessee's Democrat party. I asked to meet with the editorial board, and they graciously agreed. I took along some notes as to things I thought might persuade them to reconsider. They did.

Two days after the paper's endorsement, on 23 April 2006 the *News Sentinel* published a long story stoking the fire. As I say, David Lee and I sold a lot of papers for the *News Sentinel*:

Feud Spills into Judge Race

Last summer, David Lee told a state appeals court he wouldn't take the job if elected to the post he is running for—Knox County's 4th Circuit Court judge. . . .

Last week, Lee indicated that he wished he hadn't written that and that he intends to serve as the judge if he defeats Swann, the longtime 4th Circuit judge. "If I was more astute at politics, I would not have put that in there," Lee said. . . .

Lee and Swann are locked in a campaign battle to be judge of the unhappiest court in Knox County, and neither one is shy about saying what he believes. Last week, a reporter told Swann, who has been on the 4th Circuit bench for nearly 24 years, that some lawyers don't like him very much and consider him difficult to deal with.

"I'm a type A person who makes difficult decisions that others are afraid to make, and that will offend some people," Swann replied before talking about [a retired judge who had] never jailed anyone for the nonpayment of child support.

That judge "never made anyone mad," he said. "He would not make the hard decisions, and I don't shy away from that," Swann said, "and that is going to bruise some egos."

. . .

Lee started running against Swann as a result of Lee's own highly contentious divorce proceeding before Swann. The divorce is final, but the case remains open because of money battles.

In 2003, Lee's ex-wife filed a motion claiming an enraged Lee told her, "I want to kill you," "You're dead," and "You're gonna be really, really sorry," while calling her names in a Dec. 16, 2003, telephone call. Lee declined to comment about his divorce . . .

Two days after the election was over *News Sentinel* color columnist Sam Venable wrote, with obvious enjoyment,

> *... Bill Swann's campaign took a sure-nuff journey down Memory Lane. Swann and David Lee were embroiled in a contentious race for the 4th Circuit Court Judgeship, which Swann has held since 1982. As is typical in any particularly quarrelsome campaign, there were charges and countercharges of sign stealing. Without assessing blame either way, I gotta hand it to Swann for his innovative, humorous—and, ultimately, winning—approach to the matter. He fashioned a series of signs in the style of vintage highway advertising panels and posted them at strategic locations. An example:*

> Help us find
> The unkind mind
> Who's tearing down
> Judge Swann's signs.

> *Followed, of course, by the "Burma Shave" logo. Twenty-three skidoo! You can't get much more Yankee Doodle All-American Dandy than that.*

The final count in the Republican primary of 2006 was:

- Swann   12,735 (59.2%)
- Lee   8,779 (40.8%)

My guess is that Lee spent well over a hundred thousand dollars.

A few months later in the general election I ran unopposed, receiving 31,798 votes.

Chapter 23

SO YOU THINK POLITICS IS ABOUT CIVIL DISCOURSE?

As you have seen, I won the 2006 campaign for re-election. David Lee had been the opponent in the May Republican primary. And I had no opponent in the August general election.

What you may not know is that the primary campaign cost me $60,00, of which I was able to raise $29,000. So $31,000 of back-pocket consequences in order to be sure to defeat a strong opponent. I am not complaining. Life is not fair. However, life is as my twenty-month-old granddaughter frequently stated, "Doing, doing, doing."

Diana and I don't know if the baby is here making a statement, or perhaps delivering an exhortation, or just reveling in her newfound joy of language. But politics is certainly about continuous doing.

The 2006 campaign reached its nadir of "doing" in a moment few noticed. Few noticed because it came from "Pirate News Television," the creation of John Lee, brother of David Lee:

Swann in celebrity death match with judicial candidate David Lee, brother of PNTV producer John Lee

KNOXVILLE, Tenn. Pirate News TV censored from CTV [Knoxville's Community Television, Channel 12] for 3rd week. CTV refuses to play PNTV videotapes—no reason given.

But most likely because lawyers for Judicial candidate David Lee filed complaints against Judge Bill Swann's twice-weekly CTV show, for not providing mandatory equal time to other candidates.

But the best complaint against Swann's show is that it violated CTV contract, by repeating itself in an endless loop. Swann's CTV show, "Orders of Protection," is illegally produced by WATE [Channel 6], and by WATE talking head Gene Patterson, former "deputy mayor of propaganda" for Skull & Bones mayor/ambassador Victor "Victoria" Ashe. . . .

Swann also produces his entire CTV show while speaking Spanish, to recruit illegal aliens to overthrow USA, and create the criminal cannibal nation of Aztlan. This is an act of treason—a crime punishable by death.

Courthouses in Texas allow ONLY Spanish to be spoken in US courts, and the English language is BANNED. ONLY MEXICAN FLAGS are allowed to be displayed at those courthouses in USA. All across USA, US flags are banned at US Schools, in order to overthrow the US Constitution, and to overthrow USA.

If you want to overthrow USA, then vote for Bill Swann for judge . . . But if you want to live in America, and speak English, and have a job, and not live in a Police State Gulag slave plantation, then vote for David Lee.

As you can see, civil discourse was not the goal of this news release, nor even truth.

The 2006 campaign was a battle from beginning to end. My opponent was extremely able, a Vanderbilt graduate, well-funded, more attractive than I on television, and articulate. Happily, the Republican primary ended his candidacy.

But the battle wasn't over when it was over. It lived on in the lawsuit *Rose v. Swann*, filed by Wendy Rose, one of David Lee's strong and able campaign operatives.

Chapter 24

ROSE v. SWANN

In his election campaign to replace me, David Lee worked hard. And he was fortunate to have a hard-working, intelligent campaign operative, Wendy Rose.

She and two other women who had litigated in Fourth Circuit Court appeared in a glossy, eight-page, full-color David Lee campaign piece detailing to the world how I had gotten their cases wrong, and therefore should not be re-elected. The eight-page flyers were handed out, I am told, at every Pilot and Weigel's convenience market in Knox County, and, I understand, inserted into newspapers.

After her divorce, Wendy Rose had remarried. As it happened, she married a lawyer. Through her new husband she filed a tort lawsuit, *Rose v. Swann,* claiming that I had defamed her in my election campaign against David Lee, and that accordingly she should be awarded damages of one million dollars.

The lawsuit sounded in libel and slander; defamation of character; intentional infliction of emotional distress; outrageous conduct; and violation of civil rights under Title 42, Section 1983, of the United States Code.

I was alleged to have done all this during the hurly-burly of the 2006 campaign. Paragraph 26 of her complaint states that Swann (the Defendant) "also knew, or should have known, that

93

the libelous statements he made regarding the Plaintiff . . . would humiliate the Plaintiff, cause severe damage to her personal and professional reputation and would most likely ruin her insurance business known as Innovative Insurance Group, L.L.C."

Wendy Rose's lawsuit centered on three words she attributed to me:

- "sleazy,"
- "ludicrous," and
- "liar."

The first word, "sleazy," was indeed spoken by me, in a television interview. I characterized David Lee's entire campaign as sleazy, but not Wendy Rose herself.

The second word, "ludicrous," was also spoken by me, and it was printed by a newspaper reporter. I had said that it was "ludicrous" to suggest I rushed through trials when in fact my own Knox County clerks frequently told me I was too patient, letting hearings wind down to their own leisurely conclusions.

The third word ("liar") was never spoken by anyone, certainly not by me, but Wendy Rose here apparently refers to a campaign letter from lawyers supporting me. They urged voters not to be deceived by "half-truths" published by David Lee.

If you want, you can reflect upon the intrinsic merit of this litigation by reading Judge Wheeler Rosenbalm's final order and incorporated memorandum opinion. [ENDNOTES 1 AND 2] The opinion was an excellent outcome, the final and much delayed event in a sadness of many years' duration.

It is a cliché to say that civil litigation frequently takes forever. (In fact, civil litigation takes so long that, given a choice, businessmen will mediate rather than litigate. There's a chapter in this book about that.)

Clichés are clichés because they are true. *Rose v. Swann* lasted almost six years, from 8 September 2006 to 22 June 2012 (the thirty-first day after entry of Judge Rosenbalm's 21 May 2012 final order). And I still had attorney fees afterwards.

As I say, life's not fair. I urge you, dear reader, to do the right thing even when there may be adverse consequences for you. [ENDNOTE 3]

But *Rose v. Swann* is about more than the hurly-burly of politics, more than the give-and-take of political discourse. The filing and pursuit of this sort of lawsuit stands as an example of evil at work in our world.

When I speak of "evil" here, I don't mean the obviously "bad things" that occur in life—the child hit by the car on a city street, hurricanes causing death and property damage. As far as we know, those are random bad things. I am speaking theologically. I mean a conscious force which acts directly and intentionally, or intentionally finds expression through its handmaidens.

This theological evil, like unfairness, is in my opinion simply a fact of life. It is not often spoken of. It is not fashionable to do so. But I speak of it to you so that you will be alert. It's just the way it is.

I encountered theological evil looking for a target, looking for a way to express itself. It is the roaring lion of 1 Peter 5, prowling about looking for someone to devour.

I believe there are several things here to think about:

- First, there are bad people in life. If they decide to target you, if they decide to look for a chink in your armor, it is because they want to hurt you. Some do it because they are evil; some do it for entertainment. Some do it for monetary gain where that is a possibility for them.
- Second, you, dear reader, should always have the courage to do the right thing, even if the consequences may be adverse for you. [ENDNOTE 3]

- Third, if the consequences in fact turn out to be adverse, that does not prove you made the wrong decision. It is merely proof that life is not fair.
- Fourth, do not expect life to be fair. Expect adversity; deal with it skillfully, as skillfully as you can, so that you can reduce the negative impact.

Chapter 25

BUCHENWALD

Last year I published three short pieces on the Holocaust. They were chapters 10, 11, and 19 in *Five Proofs of Christianity* (Westbow Press, 2016). I called them "Beech Forest" pieces, using the English "beech" for *Buchen* (beech trees) and "forest" for *Wald*. You probably recognize *Wald* from black forest cake (*Schwarzwaldtorte),* or waldorf salad, or simply from the black forest itself (*Schwarzwald).*

No one should write short pieces about the Holocaust. We should only write encyclopedias. Volumes. Thick books on the depth and multiplicity of evil displayed 1933-45 in the Third Reich. The horror of civilization gone awry, the abject shame of the German people, the loss of the Enlightenment, the descent into decadent debasement. No short pieces on the Holocaust, unless they be graven on granite monuments. No short pieces on man's inhumanity to man. No business as usual, ever again.

When a primitive people engages in genocide, it seems to do it from hatred, or territorial lust, or just from received prejudice. When a civilized people—the Germans, the Austrians (but not the Swiss Germans!)—devolve into genocide, they seem to do it from received prejudice, or willful inattention, or sloth. And the killers-on-point (the trigger men, the railroad car loaders, the poison gas releasers) appear to do it from cruelty, from sadism, or simply from a desire to be unnoticed within the larger system. "I'm just following orders."

"How can this be?" you ask. You say, "I could never do it. I could never have done it." Really? How sure are you? How sure am I? How good are we really? My prayer, dear reader, is that both of us are very, very firm in our morality.

Yet we are told that 'everyone' breaks under torture. 'Everyone' will betray his country, his nation's secrets. 'Everyone' will give more than name, rank, and serial number—in fact will gushingly give up everything to stop the pain of torture. "Don't do it to me!" screams Winston Smith. "Do it to Julia!"—his beloved.

Elie Wiesel in his 1986 Nobel Peace Prize acceptance said that he swore not to be one of those who went along with the system:

> . . . I swore never to be silent whenever and wherever human beings endure suffering and humiliation. We must always take sides. Neutrality helps the oppressor, never the victim. Silence encourages the tormentor, never the tormented . . . When human lives are endangered, when human dignity is in jeopardy, national borders and sensitivities become irrelevant. Wherever men or women are persecuted because of their race, religion, or political views, that place must—at that moment—become the center of the universe.

The center of the universe. If that is so, where is the center of our universe today?

I say it is in every Arab land where Christians are persecuted, beheaded, shot, burned; where girls are kidnapped into sex slavery; where the Christian Copts are hunted down for worshipping Jesus; where schoolgirls are attacked for learning Western ways. The center of the universe is in every gathering of gays in the US attacked by Arabs, by ISIS, by any of the on-site boneheads *du jour*. It is next door to us.

And not to speak is to speak, not to act is to act, as Dietrich Bonhoeffer taught us—Bonhoeffer who first came to the attention of the National Democratic Socialist Workers Party by opposing Hitler's 'mercy killing' of the mentally infirm, who continued attracting the attention of the Party by his active Protestantism, by his Jewish brother-in-law, and finally by his complicity in the plot to kill Hitler.

Bonhoeffer who returned from the safety of New York City to his Germany, refusing to be absent from Germany in her hour of need. He returned to the center of his universe:

> *I have made a mistake in coming to America. I must live through this difficult period in our national history with the Christian people of Germany. I will have no right to participate in the reconstruction of Christian life in Germany after the war if I do not share the trials of this time with my people.*

Our center of the universe is in every Arab land:

- where Sunnis kill Shiites because they are Shiites,
- where Shiites kill Sunnis because they are Sunnis,
- where Sunnis kill Sunnis because they are apostate Sunnis.

Our center of the universe is is also:

- In Orlando 12 June 2016 (ISIS-pledged Omar Mateen kills forty-nine gays);
- In Berlin 19 December 2016, the Christmas Market (ISIS-pledged Anis Amri kills twelve and injures fifty);
- In our town, in casual slurs;
- It is wherever hatred abounds.

Chapter 26

MEDIATION AND LITIGATION

A bit more on politics. Businessmen do not litigate.

They have better things to do. They mediate. They have a businesses to run. They cannot waste months in trial preparation and then a week or more in the trial itself. And then possibly waste more time on post-trial motions and appeals. Not to speak of the money spent on attorney fees and court costs.

No. There are sales to make, contracts to sign, loans to secure. Litigation is paralysis.

There are five factors I think which can tell you whether a case can be settled by mediation, or by good attorneys in pretrial negotiations. Let us imagine a simple case of only two parties.

- If one of the parties is mean and petty, that is <u>a score of one</u>. The case can probably be settled by mediation or, as I say, by good attorneys in pretrial negotiations.
- If one of the parties is mean and greedy for money, the case has <u>a score of two</u>, and can probably be settled, but only with money.
- If one person additionally has a firm belief the other side is a truly bad person, <u>the case is a three</u> and can only be settled with money and self-abasement.

- If one person is mean, money-greedy, morally superior, and additionally has a "by God . . ." attitude, the case must be litigated. <u>It is a four,</u> and it is a mess.
- The fifth and last factor is the presence of a combative attorney. I mean more than a zealous, devoted, and competent attorney. Each side hopefully has that. I mean an attorney who fights because of his own personality deficiencies. Who needs to show off, perhaps. Or who is so insecure he needs to sneer, preen, and triumph. With this sort of attorney, <u>the case is a five,</u> and only a judge can sort it out.

Chapter 27

CRONY CAPITALISM AND SPECIAL INTERESTS: A PRIMER IN GRIEVANCE

"Crony capitalism" is not just another one of the many "isms." It is not just a fashionable pursuit which is here today and gone tomorrow. It is not, as many "isms" are, just a buzzword populating a given political cycle.

Crony capitalism is the way things are. It is the way things work.

Wait now: I am not an apologist for this terrible "-ism." Quite the opposite: I hold crony capitalism to be a dispiriting, enervating, gut-ripping assault on fair dealing. Whenever there is insider influence in government, Adam Smith's invisible hand is without fingers.

Crony capitalism—a system intended to benefit those close to government policy makers—promotes envy, hatred, "us-versus-them" thinking, and the oft-heard observation, "The system is rigged." Because of course it is rigged. It's the way things work.

Be patient with me here. I have a solution, maybe. Yes, let's concede the system is "rigged," in the sense that there are persons who want, and who get, their projects disproportionately advanced by government and thereby they profit handsomely.

This advancement need not be just the limited favoring of an "innovative" startup tech company—e.g., Solyndra—with loans guaranteed by the government, followed by government hiding of negative information about Solyndra.

The rigging of the system can be, and often is, for an entire sector of business—say, Midwestern agriculture, which is favored by a government policy promoting ethanol. Here an entire horde of "special interests" gets the benefits—farmers, grain elevator operators, railroads taking corn to refineries, petrochemical engineers, and so on.

But these people aren't "special." They are just identifiable, just good, regular Americans who are identified by what they do.

"Special interests" is a dirty term in political-speak. It should not be. It merely means, as I say, "identifiable by task."

But when I think someone is getting more than I do in profit and/or insider status, I am resentful. I want him yanked up and shamed, root and branch. And frankly, he should be, if you believe in unfettered, freely operating capitalism which, without insider help, evaluates and adjusts prices for risk and reward. The invisible hand. But when the invisible hand is grabbed by government and bent backward, you get Solyndra, or whatever the latest insider outrage is named.

And there you have it. We descend into vitriol, even protests perhaps, and the media fills its twenty-four-hour news cycle with the protests. This gives us a new grievance in a society already bloated with grievances.

"Americans Against Ethanol" (AAE) is countered by "Americans For Ethanol" (AFE). Each of the pressure groups finances think tanks, hires K-Street lobbyists, and off we go, AAE and AFE, wasting our time and attention on derivative issues.

Inevitable? Perhaps. Or definitely inevitable, if politics is nothing more than the way Ambrose Bierce (1842-1914) defined it, "a strife of interests masquerading as a contest of principles. The conduct of public affairs for private advantage." Bierce, a journalist for the Hearst corporation, regularly attacked inside dealing before the rise of the term "crony capitalism."

Bierce saw, as we do today, that often success in business depends on close ties between business persons and government persons. There is often favoritism in the passing out of legal permits, government grants, the Solyndra loan guarantees, tax breaks, and other kinds of state intervention in the normal operation of markets.

All people in business are self-serving. They should be. But when friendships and political or family ties figure in, there can be and often is corruption of economic ideals.

It can be as simple as a gentle collusion among market players tolerated or even encouraged by government. For example, an industry trade group will present a united front to government, requesting subsidies, or aid, or regulation. If government recognizes that trade group as legitimate, then any new arrivals in the market will find it difficult to enter commerce on a level footing. Or the trade group, with the blessing of government, will expand the training and certification exams necessary for newcomers to enter the market.

Crony capitalism has existed at least since the 1600s. *The Economist* has a "crony-capitalism index" which found that in 2014 the leading countries for crony influence were Hong Kong, Russia, and Malaysia. We are not alone. We are not even first.

So then is the situation hopeless? No, not if we deconstruct it. Not if we take each economics-driven gripe about favoritism back to its origin. Take ethanol for example: America had a lot of corn, often too much corn. Prices for corn fluctuated widely, putting farmers at risk, because of

- ever-changing supply and demand;
- variations in export prices;

- weather;
- and the flights of bluebirds on Tuesday mornings.

At the same time, America had wildly fluctuating gasoline prices, due to bad (that is to say, "foreign") people in the Middle East, putting consumers at risk because of

- ever-changing supply and demand;
- environmental interventions;
- other regulations;
- and the flights of goldfinches on Wednesday mornings.

Therefore, some bright, well-meaning person said, "Wouldn't it be good if a certain amount of corn were converted to fuel each year? That way we can address two problems at once. We stabilize the agricultural market somewhat with a predictable demand for corn each year, and we stabilize the fuel market somewhat with a predictable annual inflow of native-sourced fuel."

A bill in Congress and it was done. Two birds killed with one stone. Great.Then, as usually happens, the law of unintended consequences had its say.

Ethanol turns out to be harmful for certain types of engines. Ethanol is more expensive per mile driven because it is less powerful than traditional gasoline. Ethanol is inefficient. People avoid gas stations which have only ethanol-mix fuels.

But it is now too late. The programs are in place, and will be with us forever. See daylight "savings" time. "Old cowboys," we are told, "never die. They just fade away." Old government programs never die. They expand.

It takes twenty government agencies to allow a quart of milk to be sold. But don't worry about ethanol: Soon there will be a high-sounding revamp of the program, "The 2018 Patriotic Act for Home-Grown Solutions." This act, we are told, will fix it all.

But enough of ethanol. The truly classic special interests have always lived in the benign shadow of import tariffs. Tariffs are taxes paid by consumers on products entering America. In the early days of America, tariffs were the main source of revenue for the new nation.

Today, though, we hear, "Higher prices for Chinese-made widgets will help American widget makers." This is a good thing, surely. Well, yes, it is, for the domestic manufacturers of widgets and for those who supply them with the raw materials to make widgets. And, we are told, surely the American widget buyer is ready to pay "a little more" for a real American widget.

But it doesn't take tariffs, or an entire agricultural or banking sector, to get us to governmental interference with the invisible hand of capitalism. If a municipality, a state, or the federal government decides there should be a regulation mandating longer drip eaves on A-frame vacation houses ("It's a good thing, don't you know, it'll keep the siding from getting mildew."), the copper flashing lobby and the copper mining lobby will celebrate.

Now those people in the copper industry are clearly a special interest. And therefore they are bad? No, they are not; they are merely identifiable. Their self-interest is not suspect. The only correct question to ask is whether the flashing length regulation benefits the taxpayers more than it costs them.

Taxation, tariffs, and regulations have always expressed governmental policy. And always will. What we need to do, I suggest, is vet the policies very slowly and thoroughly before we enact them.

Once, in a fit of socially beneficial thinking, I believed this nation could have a mandatory sunsetting of 10% of all regulations every year. It would be prospective, of course, so as to get it through Congress, and so as not to upset the present applecart filled with copper flashing, ethanol, and widgets.

It would be simple: Every new regulation would expire in ten years unless re-enacted. (We do that now in some states in limited instances.) Such a sunsetting would of course hugely increase the national discussion of a given regulation as each sunset date approached. Lobbyists on each side would flourish. Lawyers would buy new Jaguars. But we would be enacting our own regulations, not just humbly receiving them.

Do you wonder why you flush your toilet more times now on each visit than you did years ago? It is because you are "saving water." A good goal, surely. Do you wonder why you cope with daylight savings time twice a year, putting it in and taking it out, having headaches, being tired, and resetting all your clocks? [ENDNOTE 9] It is because you are "saving energy." A good goal, surely. But the annual cost to the U.S. economy of changing our clocks is $433,982,548 according to a study cited by the *Wall Street Journal* (3 November 2016). And pedestrian deaths in the week after daylight savings time ends jumped from 65 to 227.

In fact, we are saving neither water nor energy. Government programs never go away, even when clearly a bad idea.

But to return to "special" interests: We are all special interests. That is, we are all identifiable as belonging to this or that group, and usually we have many such belongings. Our interests do not become that "dirty" thing, crony capitalism, until the costs of advancing our interests outweigh the benefits to the nation and its consumers. And that of course is the discussion.

But let's be clear: the dirty word here is "crony," not capitalism. Even dirtier than crony capitalism, and always obvious, is "crony socialism" and "crony communism." Insiders skimming the till. Socialist and communist governments, which are closed and secretive, make skimming easy. Our representative governments are open. But we trust them, pretty much, and therefore don't look at them hard enough. We don't watch them diligently. We trust, and we suffer for it.

Chapter 28

TAXATION IS THEFT

Taxation is theft. Except when it isn't. Except when I agree that some of my money may be taken to build roads and move sewage. But only this and nothing more. Well, OK, and policemen . . .

Well, I suppose national defense requires some tax support. But that's it. Nothing else . . .

Well, the enforcement of contracts is pretty important, and I guess government has to do that, and government is not free. So OK, taxation for the support of contract law . . .

Libertarians

What we are talking about here is libertarianism. As I understand today's libertarians, they accept a limited amount of government. As little as possible. Robert Nozick puts it this way:

> *The minimal state is the most extensive state that can be justified. Any state more extensive violates people's' rights.* [ENDNOTE 13]

Milton and Rose Friedman put it this way:

> *A society that puts equality—in the sense of equality of outcome—ahead of freedom will end up*

with neither equality nor freedom. The use of force ["Force" is not just physical force; it also includes taxation.] *to achieve equality will destroy freedom, and the force, introduced for good purposes, will end up in the hands of people who use it to promote their own interests.*

On the other hand, a society that puts freedom first will, as a happy by-product, end up with both greater freedom and greater equality. Though a by-product of freedom, greater equality is not an accident. A free society releases the energies and abilities of people to pursue their own objectives. [ENDNOTE 14]

Most libertarians agree that there should be:

- no paternalistic laws
- no morals legislation
- no taxation aimed at redistribution of wealth from the rich to the poor.

Let's unpack those three points somewhat.

There should be no paternalistic legislation—that which protects us from ourselves. That which looks out for our best interests, as a parent does for her children. For example, libertarians would have no seat belt laws, no helmet laws, no ban on large sugary soft drinks. (It may in fact be better for you to wear your seat belt or to wear a helmet when you ride a motorcycle, or better for you to avoid large quantities of sugary drinks, but it should be your decision. It is not for government to decide.) You are allowed to sell your body parts, and you are allowed to commit suicide.

There should also be no moral viewpoints expressed in legislation. For example, the viewpoint of a putative majority on homosexuality should not be expressed in legislation outlawing gays and lesbians.

And the libertarian says there should be no taxation for redistribution of wealth. Because to take from one to give to another is to invade the private property of the person taxed. It is a taking of his property.

Counted as an early ally of today's libertarians, John Locke had three basics: "life, liberty, and property." These were his unalienable rights, his God-given rights. [ENDNOTE FOUR] (Jefferson changed the third element from property to "the pursuit of happiness.")

For Locke, property justly acquired was untouchable by another. And a person's property includes his labor, as well as the fruits of his labor. [ENDNOTE FIVE] If someone by taxation takes your labor or the money you earned (and which you might prefer to use, for a car or a house, or a sugary drink) you are, well, a slave. Not in the classical sense, but in an extended sense. Locke emphasized that individuals matter, that individuals are distinct, that they are separate beings with separate lives worthy of respect.

A libertarian grudgingly accepts taxation for the basics of government, yes. For sewage plants, for roadways. He accepts that crime should be punished, that fraud should be prevented, that civil laws should be enforced. That a nation should be protected from outside force. So we see that libertarians have to buy into that thing which makes their very skin crawl: The State.

The dirtiest descriptive in the libertarian lexicon is "statist"— as an adjective or as a noun. As an adjective it means inclining to top-down solutions. As a noun it refers to planners who have no fear of imposing government directives on the people.

Mussolini was a statist, as are most people working in Washington today. Hitler was a statist. Communist regimes are statist. Socialist regimes are statist. Anyone who believes in top-down solutions imposed upon citizens is a statist.

Republicans tend to be less statist than Democrats, but not

by much. Conservatives on the other hand abhor state solutions, and accept them only when necessary—generally under the libertarian-permitted roles for the state—punishment of crime, enforcement of contract, national defense, and a modicum of health and welfare (traffic lights, vaccinations, water plants).

But pure libertarians get squirrely even on vaccinations and national defense. To the pure libertarians I say, "I can understand and even admire the purity of your philosophical approach, but please make some compromises, or you'll be dead. And me along with you."

It helps my tolerance that I spent thirteen years as an academic. I am accustomed to the purity of theoretical positions. All manner of gorgeous poppycock can be justified with a naive mind. Communism, socialism, free love, a stateless world.

But without national defense, only aggressive nations will survive. Mussolini, Hitler, and Putin will prevail. America will not—unless she is as aggressive in her self-defense as are the evil actors on offense against her. America had been aggressive in her self-defense until the recent eight-year spate of feckless decisions.

America was a guarantor of freedom from the end of World War Two until 2008. John Kennedy famously crystallized our responsibilities in his inaugural address 20 January 1961:

> *Let every nation know, whether it wishes us well or ill, that we shall pay any price, bear any burden, meet any hardship, support any friend, oppose any foe, in order to assure the survival and the success of liberty.*

This is American hegemony at its clearest and best. It is not imperialism, nor even cultural imperialism. It is a guaranty of our best interests, but also of the best interests of all countries seeking freedom for their people. From the Monroe Doctrine onward we have been bold to assert our sphere of influence, not to acquire land or booty, but to protect our country and its interests abroad. Jefferson himself, and later Madison, forced the Barbary pirates into submission.

You may not like a powerful America, it may make you uneasy—"Why can't we all just get along?"—but the alternative is ISIS, Putin, or learning to speak Chinese or Arabic. It's that simple.

Freedom is a most perishable flower. It requires a gun-packing gardener. Why aren't we all speaking German now? Or Japanese? Because we fought for our perishable flower.

Chapter 29

THE AGGRIEVED AND THE OTHERS

Libertarians live in rarefied air. The rest of us do not. The rest of us live often with serious political controversy. Unfortunately, we also live surrounded, always, with political babble.

Pick any political issue, and there will be two major contenders: "the aggrieved" and what I call "the others." Lately *the aggrieved* in America are found mostly on the left—often on the far left—of the political spectrum. *The others* I speak of are somewhat right of center.

As you know, I am politically conservative. But I am socially liberal. That liberal streak in me will find little expression in this chapter however, since most of what concerns me here is the give-and-take of discussion, the give-and-take of disagreement, not the issues themselves.

Americans generally incline to be conservative. That is, they oppose change and venerate tradition. If you, my reader, are usually *aggrieved* about the way things are, you probably favor "progressive," Democrat-party positions. Because you don't like the way things are, you are *aggrieved*.

In what follows here, it is crucial for us all to remember what the Reverend Bob Dannals says, in his "Inbox Inspirations":

Every encounter with another human being has the potential to be life-giving or life-diminishing. We deal out diminishment when we belittle, misunderstand, ignore, boast, and insist on our own way. We extend life when we notice, affirm, thank, and listen. [ENDNOTE 12]

This is a particularly important warning for me, because I am extremely clear in my thoughts. I know my core beliefs and I express them strongly. In so doing, I can diminish, belittle, those who disagree with me. That is not and should not be my intent. Certainly not. My intent should be to stimulate thought and discussion by clear articulation of where I stand. I must be careful.

Here is an unhappy thing: *The aggrieved* and conservatives do not play by the same rules. Most of *the aggrieved* are willing to lie, in fact are eager to lie, if those lies will aid the so-called "resistance" to President Trump.

Those lies invented by *the aggrieved* flourish and blossom because the media have ceased to be journalists (definition: reporters of the "who, what, where, when, and why"). The media have ceased being journalists and have instead become mouthpieces and advocates of the resistance. They are the agitprop of the Democrat Party.

So now the crucial question: Do conservatives lie? Well, yes: individuals among them sometimes do. But as a general rule conservatives do not lie in political discussions. Because facts matter to conservatives. Conservatives love true journalists, unbiased journalists. Journalists who insist on facts. Who discuss reality from a basis of fact. The clearest distinction between *the aggrieved* and conservatives is that the loudest of the *aggrieved* are completely comfortable with falsehoods.

A small case in point occurred three weeks into the presidency of Donald Trump. *The aggrieved* mainstream media suddenly 'recognized' that American unemployment is more accurately described by using the Bureau of Labor Statistics U-6 number, not the U-3 number.

Both numbers had always been available, but for the previous eight years the Democrat-friendly media had used the U-3 number. The U-3 number is artificially low because it omits persons who have given up looking for work. (If you have despaired, it seems, you are not unemployed.) Now suddenly the mainstream media 'recognized' that the U-6 number is more accurate and decided to use it. [ENDNOTE 10]

My point is this: The previous use of the U-3 number was a gentle falsehood. It was justifiable for *the aggrieved* to use the gentle falsehood because ends justify means. Put another way, the given cause (making the Obama administration look better on unemployment) is greater than accurate facts.

Whenever it is needed, facts may quite properly be bent to the good of the cause. It was acceptable for Dan Rather and Mary Mapes to falsify George W. Bush's biography because he had to be defeated. Mapes and Rather got caught and lost their CBS jobs, but eleven years later a revisionist history began because, don't you see, the actual facts don't really matter. Mapes's and Rather's intentions were noble.

Since Donald H.Trump became a candidate, then president-elect, then president, reporters' opinions have become acceptable additions to "news" stories. The "who, what, where, when, and why" are not enough. President Trump must additionally be called a liar and charlatan as part of the "news"story.

"Protesters" can shut down free speech on the Harvard campus, the Yale campus, the Berkeley campus, and that is fine, don't you see, because protest is good, we are told by the media. It is protected by the First Amendment. It is fundamentally American.

However, the media have no need to report that some of those so-called "protesters" were paid to do so, and that at Berkeley the paid black-clad mob destroyed property and set fires, in order to achieve the cancellation of a long-scheduled, opposed speech. Contrary ideas are not to be protected at Berkeley.

It does not matter to most of *the aggrieved* whether they tell the truth or not. Because they are convinced they are right, truth is an acceptable casualty. No conservative will knowingly take a position unsupported by fact, unsupported by truth. (Opinion is another matter. A conservative will have opinions, maybe not firmly based in fact, but will hopefully specify when arguing from fact and when arguing from mere spleen.)

The aggrieved are cosseted by the mainstream media, which finds grievance more interesting and more worthy of coverage than solutions. Thus the media choose to support a rising spiral of validation won through denunciation.

The media are spoon-fed leaks from federal bureaucracy members who are opposed to the president. As Kimberly Strassel puts it in the *Wall Street Journal,* 7 July 2017: there is "a leak crime wave, run by a bureaucratic underworld that is happy to harm U.S. interests if it maims a president."

Many of *the aggrieved* are suspicious of hard work. Or if not suspicious, they are neutral about it. Hard work for *the aggrieved* is an optional approach to life, fully as valid as welfare.

The aggrieved are always opportunistic ("Never waste a tragedy"), always eager to spring. This eagerness produces sloppy logic and sloppy reasoning, but that's acceptable because the intentions are good.

The aggrieved deny that *the others* are accomplishing anything worth doing. Alternatively, they declare that *the others* are actually harmful. This is the belittlement, the diminishment, of which Rev. Dannals speaks.

The aggrieved are out for themselves, and proud to state it. They are unconcerned for the goals of *the others*, if not actually opposed to them. See Berkeley. See Yale. See Harvard. Because they believe they have been wronged, *the aggrieved* believe they are entitled to pay-back.

The aggrieved know *the others* "have it all wrong," or sufficiently wrong that they should be removed from power.

The aggrieved actually believe *the others* to be immoral. This is the belittlement, the diminishment, of which Dannals speaks.

Now let's look at the opposite side. What are the characteristics of *the others*, the conservatives? *The others* are truthful, as I have cautiously said. When you argue with conservatives, you can change their minds with facts. This will not upset them. In fact, they will be grateful to be corrected. Surprised perhaps, but grateful.

Conservatives are usually frugal, "waste-not want-not" types. They are opposed to all misuse of resources—environmental, corporate, or governmental. They recognize that resources are finite. That one man's social welfare program equals another man's taxation. Therefore *the others* demand that any social welfare program be effective. "Good intentions" are not enough.

The others are usually religious. This may be from upbringing, but I suspect a large part of it is that *the others* have an openness to majesty, A recognition of their own smallness.

The others are uninteresting to the mainstream media. You will wait in vain to hear this: "And now let us speak about truthful, satisfied, religious, hard working people."

FAITH

Chapter 30

THE TEMPLE OF THE LORD

God gave us these temples we live in:

> . . . *do you not know that your body is a temple of the Holy Spirit within you, whom you have from God? You are not your own, for you were bought with a price. So glorify God in your body.*
>
> 1 Corinthians 6:19-20

We received these temples as gifts. They are on loan to us, for our use until we move on. Our bodies are where we live.

Whoever you are, whatever it is which makes you your particular "you"—different from John Jones, different from Nancy Smith—is trapped for now inside a corporeal frame. If you mistreat that frame, your body, then probably your uniqueness, your mental situation, is in bad shape also.

Treat your body well or ill, and you treat your mind well or ill also. Your mind is trailer-hitched to your body. At least it usually is. Your outlook, your attitude, the way you treat others, usually goes where your body goes. Again, this is not always so.

Treat your body ill, and your mental day will be an affliction to be endured, an endless series of self-reproaches. And particularly so if you are the culprit who has brought the physical woe upon yourself. But treat your body well and your day will be a joy. You will, I hope, have the inclination to pray unceasingly, as Paul says, in thanks for your joy:

> *Rejoice always, pray without ceasing, give thanks in all circumstances; for this is the will of God in Christ Jesus for you.*
>
> 1 Thessalonians 5:16-18

> *Rejoice in the Lord always; again I will say, rejoice. Let your reasonableness be known to everyone. The Lord is at hand; do not be anxious about anything, but in everything by prayer and supplication with thanksgiving let your requests be made known to God.*
>
> Philippians 4:4-6

A simple piece of Christian decorative art has three words stacked in brass upon each other:

JOY

HOPE

PEACE

We could reflect for hours on the interrelationships here: Causality: does each piece cause the next or does it follow from it? Are the three states a continuous loop, with "*peace*" preceding "*joy*" and following "*hope*"? Which came first? Could one be omitted? Other questions might occur to us as we ponder.

My point in mentioning this simple piece of art in connection with the temple of the Lord is this: When the body, the temple, is tended prayerfully, it produces joy. And peace. And the hope of many recurrences.

But your own experience has told you this already. When

you feel good, you appreciate the beauty of the dandelion and the song of the sparrow. You cherish the grey dawn, the fog gently lifting off the lake. But when you are not living in this happy zone—to borrow a dieting buzz word from Barry Sears—you are out of sorts, deaf to the birdsong, blind to the dawn. The lawn dandelions are just those weeds that you must eventually get to, a task to be addressed, not yellow splendor.

Ah, but the dandelion is a thing of beauty. A miracle. It is perfection from bud to bloom, and then it becomes something even better—a feather puffball.

Someone named dandelions "children's clocks"—a delightful, fanciful, joy-filled name. If dandelions were rare, we would order them from the Breck's catalog, grow them from seed, give them to friends and neighbors. The French call them "wet the bed" plants, *pissenlit*, for their diuretic properties. Silly people. But we know the dandelion as the true tooth of the lion, God's gift, Aslan's tooth.

In Psalm 51 David prays for a clean heart, an upright spirit:

> *Create in me a clean heart, O God,*
> *and renew a right spirit within me.*
> *Cast me not away from your presence,*
> *and take not your Holy Spirit from me.*
> *Restore to me the joy of your salvation,*
> *and uphold me with a willing spirit.*

David could equally well have prayed for his body, his loaned temple of the Lord, to be clean and pure, that he might live well in it, not ill. That he might rejoice in dandelions.

Paul tells us in Romans 8:1-5 that we can have the peace which David prays for, that we can be free of the devil's foot soldiers, because there is no condemnation—even self-inflicted condemnation—for those who are in Christ. God set aside the

record of debt which stood against us, nailing it to the cross.
(Colossians 2:14)

Every day in the temple is a gift from the Lord God; each day lived well in the temple is a gift back to God.

> *Do you not know that you are God's Temple and that God's spirit dwells in you? If anyone destroys God's temple, God will destroy him. For God's temple is holy, and you are that temple.*
>
> *1 Corinthians 3:16-17*

Now the bad news. We have a problem, don't we? There is that tricky and difficult matter of becoming accustomed to the privilege of joy. Complacency.

There you are, there I am, in the moment, in the midst of a joyful day, or in the midst of a series of days well spent. There we are, living in the zone of kind thoughts, good nutrition, not too many french fries, not too much red wine, no Bathsheba.

And then we stop relishing our wellness, our physical and mental health. We stop looking at the dandelions, stop noticing our devotion to God, and then . . . And then because we are not praying unceasingly, the foot soldiers of the evil one sneak in.

They ambush us. We have gone to sleep on the battlements. We no longer aspire to protect and cherish the temple of the Lord. We are coarse, like the porter in *Macbeth*, who tardily answers Macduff's pounding on the castle door:

> **Macduff.** *Was it so late, friend, ere you went to bed, That you do lie so late?*
> **Porter.** *'Faith sir, we were carousing till the second cock: and drink, sir, is a great provoker of three things.*
> **Macduff.** *What three things does drink especially provoke?*

Porter. Marry, sir, nose-painting, sleep, and urine.

Act II, Scene 3

The foot soldiers whisper to us, "Clean living, praying unceasingly, that gets boring. It gets old. Right? You've been there, done that. You have other things to do now." Then the foot soldiers escalate their assault. They bring out the longbows and a catapult: "It is time to move on, move onward to new territory. Enough with enjoying present achievements. What counts is what you have yet to do."

Eternal dissatisfaction with the present, the foot soldiers tell you, is a man's badge of honor. You are to press on. And then they add, "Besides, you deserve to relax. Forget all that silly stuff in Peter's letter:

> *Humble yourselves, therefore, under the mighty hand of God so that at the proper time he may exalt you, casting all your anxieties on him, because he cares for you. Be sober-minded; be watchful. Your adversary the devil prowls around like a roaring lion, seeking someone to devour. Resist him, firm in your faith, knowing that the same kinds of suffering are being experienced by your brotherhood throughout the world. And after you have suffered a little while, the God of all grace, who has called you to his eternal glory in Christ, will himself restore, confirm, strengthen, and establish you.*
>
> *1 Peter 5:6-9*

Forget all that stuff," the foot soldiers say. "It is outdated."

What do the foot soldiers want you to forget? They want you to forget the beauty of the dandelions, forget that there is an adversary, forget that the lion is prowling, forget that the adversary seeks you, forget that you are at risk.

David wants to be sober-minded and watchful. He is on his knees, he is weeping: "Create in me a clean heart, O God . . ." Ah, but the evil lion tells us that David's prayer is just self-centered drivel. The foot soldiers of the roaring lion whisper to us, just when we are doing our best, just in our success of living in the zone, just when we are praying unceasingly.

They whisper: "You know very well you are not clean, never will be. You are a fraud, soon to be discovered. You'd best keep working furiously, so that at least others continue to be deceived. So that you can feel the satisfaction of hard labor."

The foot soldiers sing to us in chorus, "At least you tried hard, gave it your all. It's time to give it a rest." Then they add, sneakily, ". . . and you got to eat a lot of french fries and drink a lot of red wine. Which you richly deserved, by the way. And Bathsheba was pretty much fun, right?"

Is it fair that I link spiritual health and physical health? Yes, it is fair, if your physical health is/was within your voluntary control. Certainly we know that if you damage your physical health with too much queso dip and margaritas you will be bloated and have a hangover. Those are voluntary choices.

If you make those your choices, your mind will suffer along with your body. We know that if you get an STD from Bathsheba, your mind will follow your physical woes long after doxycycline abates the symptoms. Quite aside from the guilt.

If we take the long view here, it seems that our temple of the Lord is designed to have both physical health and spiritual health simultaneously. But it can have either alone. Or it can have neither.

When we have both physical health and spiritual health, we are in the zone of joy I spoke of above—the glorious zone where you are in danger of becoming complacent, in danger of becoming oblivious to your joy. We can fall out of that zone willfully, but most usually we do it by spiritual or physical sloth. The foot soldiers traffic best in complacency: "You are trying too hard. It is time to stop praying."

Now, a hard truth: Through no fault of your own, the temple you have may be one which has weak, broken battlements and holes in its walls. But it is still your temple, still your gift to and from God. Your task is still joy, but your task is immeasurably harder than the task of most people, the task of the complacent victors: They only have to stay awake, praying unceasingly.

You, however, hurt all the time. You have six oral medications a day, three injections a day, therapy twice a week, and no left foot. It is harder to live with joy in your temple. But you do it somehow. As you do it, you inspire us all. And you dance before God.

Make no mistake: You can live in joy in the temple of the Lord even without physical health, if the absence of physical health is not of your own doing—if you have not been complicit in the loss of your physical health. But if you destroyed your body with voluntary choices, joy will be hard or impossible to find.

Another possibility exists: people who do have physical health but no spiritual health. Their bodies are not temples to the Lord, only undeserved gifts from the Lord—at least, so it appears to us:

> *But I say to you, love your enemies and pray for those who persecute you, so that you may be sons of your Father who is in heaven. For he makes his sun rise on the evil and on the good, and sends rain on the just and on the unjust.*
>
> *Matthew 5:44-45*

> *Again I saw that under the sun the race is not to the swift, nor the battle to the strong, nor bread to the wise, nor riches to the intelligent, nor favor to those with knowledge, but time and chance happen to them all.*
>
> *Ecclesiastes 9:11*

An old gospel song sets out the problem:

Tempted and tried, we're oft made to wonder
Why it should be thus all the day long;
While there are others living about us,
Never molested, though in the wrong.

Farther along we'll know more about it,
Farther along we'll understand why;
Cheer up, my brother, live in the sunshine,
We'll understand it all by and by.

Sometimes I wonder why I must suffer,
Go in the rain, the cold, and the snow,
When there are many living in comfort,
Giving no heed to all I can do.

Tempted and tried, how often we question
Why we must suffer year after year,
Being accused by those of our loved ones,
E'en though we've walked in God's holy fear.

Often when death has taken our loved ones,
Leaving our home so lone and so drear,
Then do we wonder why others prosper,
Living so wicked year after year.
Public domain, W.B. Stevens, 1911

And lastly, there are the persons whose bodies, whose temples, have neither spiritual nor physical health. This is the toughest of the permutations, the bleakest and the saddest. But even worse, another possibility exists if the absence of physical health is reversible—for example, a drug addiction, obesity, nicotine dependency—and the sufferer chooses not to reverse it. He is truly lost in a world of excuses and self deception.

Those are at least some of the permutations of life in the Lord's temple, as it seems to me. In one of C.S. Lewis's best known passages, he speaks of health:

> *There are only two kinds of people in the end: those who say to God, <u>Thy</u> will be done, and those to whom God says, in the end, <u>Thy</u> will be done.*
> *All that are in Hell, choose it. Without that self choice there could be no Hell. No soul that seriously and constantly desires joy will ever miss it. Those who seek find. To those who knock it is opened.*
> —The Great Divorce
Geoffrey Bles (UK), 1945

This is hard stuff: God will let you go, will give you over to the darkness if you choose it. Paul states in Romans 1:28:

> *And since they did not see fit to acknowledge God, God gave them up to a debased mind to do what ought not to be done. They were filled with all manner of unrighteousness, evil, covetousness, malice.*

This is not God's wish. It is the opposite of his will. Christ makes this beautifully plain to us in two of his parables:

> *So he told them this parable: "What man of you, having a hundred sheep, if he has lost one of them, does not leave the ninety-nine in the open country, and go after the one that is lost, until he finds it?*

And when he has found it, he lays it on his shoulders, rejoicing. And when he comes home, he calls together his friends and his neighbors, saying to them, 'Rejoice with me, for I have found my sheep that was lost.'

Just so, I tell you, there will be more joy in heaven over one sinner who repents than over ninety-nine righteous persons who need no repentance.

"Or what woman, having ten silver coins, if she loses one coin, does not light a lamp and sweep the house and seek diligently until she finds it?

And when she has found it, she calls together her friends and neighbors, saying, 'Rejoice with me, for I have found the coin that I had lost.'

Just so, I tell you, there is joy before the angels of God over one sinner who repents." (Emphasis mine.)

Luke 15:3-10

It is a curiosity of our nature that we think a lot about our own efforts to find God—we are proud of our study, our prayer, our works perhaps—and we fail to note that when *we* find God, it is often just the opposite. God has found *us*. God has pursued us and caught us, blessed us, raised us up, cherished us. And we thought it was our doing all along. The rooster in the morning believes he has crowed up the sun.

But God will also give us over, wash his hands of us, if we steadfastly deny him.

Chapter 31

JOHN UPDIKE: SEVEN STANZAS AT EASTER

I wrote some lines earlier in *Five Proofs of Christianity* (WestBow, 2016):

> *I know as a Christian that Easter is our bedrock. Thirty-three years after the birth of Christ the resurrection occurred, without which, as Paul says, we are nowhere. Our hope is in vain. And we are of all people most to be pitied because we have believed in vain. Easter is for me a coldly rational, magnificent moment.*

Perhaps I was wrong. Easter need not be a coldly rational moment, at least not from John Updike's perspective. It is a monstrous, shocking moment, literally true in its screamingly scientific detail; impossible, but true. It is not to be toned down, rationalized, prettified. It is to be confronted and accepted, or confronted and fled. There is no compromise:

> *Make no mistake: if He rose at all*
> *it was as His body;*

if the cells' dissolution did not reverse, the molecules
reknit, the amino acids rekindle,
the Church will fall.

Christ rose from the grave, Updike says, with the same hinged thumbs and toes we ourselves have, the same valved heart we have—but with Christ it was a heart that had been pierced, a heart that died, that withered, and then regathered new strength.

Let us not mock God with metaphor,
analogy, sidestepping, transcendence;
making of the event a parable . . .
—*Telephone Poles and Other Poems*
New York: Alfred A. Knopf, 1963

No, says Updike, it is Christ himself, body reconstituted, raised from the dead, who emerges when the stone is rolled back. A real stone, the same stone which for each of us will someday eclipse our own wide light of day, just as it did for Christ.

John Updike (1932-2009) wrote this thirty-five line poem in 1960 while attending a Lutheran congregation in Marblehead, Massachusetts. He entered it in the church's poetry competition, won its hundred-dollar prize, and gave the money back to the congregation.

He was twenty-eight years old and already wise enough to see, as many gospel singers do, the view from inside the cave, the end of our daylight, approaching death, "the vast rock of materiality that in the slow grinding of time will eclipse for each of us the wide light of day."

This is the visceral clarity Jamie Dailey and Darrin Vincent deal out in "By the Mark," a new gospel song.

More than fifty years have passed since Updike wrote his poem, and still it drives our thoughts. It makes us decide. This is poetry in action. Christ is for real, or he isn't. We must decide.

Here is the text of "By the Mark," a gospel treatment of Updike's physical images:

When I cross over
I will shout and sing.
I will know my savior
By the mark where the
Nails have been,
By the sign
(deep in his side)
Upon his precious skin.

I will know my savior
When I come to him
By the mark where the
Nails have been.

A man of riches
May claim a crown of jewels,
But the king of heaven
Can be told from the
Prince of fools
By the mark where the
Nails have been.

—*Gillian Welch, 1996, Revival*

I find this gospel song powerful. Why do I react with deep emotion to these sung lines? If you are a believing, studying Christian you will know that the theology is sound on both the points made:

- *Only Christ's sacrifice and resurrection save us from finitude. Only his gift and his miracle can give us hope of forgiveness, hope of reconciliation to God, hope of more than this life.*

- *The prince of fools is both the devil ("the father of lies"— John 8:44) and the rich man with his crown of jewels. We can blindly walk the road of folly if we choose, but we can easily recognize the king of heaven.*

Fine. There is certainly valid theology here, as there is in most gospel music. But this particular gospel song finds me where I live. Probably my emotional reception springs from my own need to hear the message.

Chapter 32

YOUR GRANDMOTHER

Where is that grandmother now—or perhaps for you it was a grandfather—where is that grandparent who meant so much to you? Who was a person you thought wise beyond words, who understood life, and who taught you the importance of what you did by example? Who taught you to make chocolate donuts and to plant a rock garden?

Where is that mother now, that grandmother's daughter, who was so poor as a child that for her at Christmas one real orange was a magical gift? [ENDNOTE 7]

They are in heaven, surely, with the saints, if there is a heaven and if there are saints.

> *Oh, come now, angel band,*
> *Come and around me stand,*
> *Oh, bear me away on your snow white wings*
> *To my immortal home.*
> —*The Stanley Brothers and the*
> *Clinch Mountain Boys,*
> *"Angel Band,"*
> *The Complete Mercury Recordings,*
> *2003, Mercury*

But there is one promise that is given—
I'll meet you on God's golden shore.
                              —Dick Burnett, *"I Am A Man of*
                                        Constant Sorrow"
                              1913, public domain

Paul tells us in 1 Thessalonians 4:13-18 that we will be reunited:

But we do not want you to be uninformed, brothers,
about those who are asleep, that you may not grieve
as others do who have no hope. For since we believe
that Jesus died and rose again, even so, through
Jesus, God will bring with him those who have
fallen asleep.
For this we declare to you by a word from the Lord,
that we who are alive, who are left until the coming
of the Lord, will not precede those who have fallen
asleep. For the Lord himself will descend from
heaven with a cry of command, with the voice of
an archangel, and with the sound of the trumpet of
God. And the dead in Christ will rise first.
Then we who are alive, who are left, will be caught
up together with them in the clouds to meet the
Lord in the air, and so we will always be with the
Lord. Therefore encourage one another with these
words.

Christ tells us of heaven as well:

One of the criminals who were hanged railed at
him, saying, "Are you not the Christ? Save yourself
and us!"
But the other rebuked him, saying, "Do you not
fear God, since you are under the same sentence

*of condemnation? And we indeed justly, for we are
receiving the due reward of our deeds; but this man
has done nothing wrong."*

*And he said, "Jesus, remember me when you come
into your kingdom."*

*And he said to him, "Truly, I say to you, today you
will be with me in Paradise."* (Luke 23:39-43)

And again:

*Let not your hearts be troubled. Believe in God;
believe also in me. In my Father's house are many
rooms. If it were not so, would I have told you that
I go to prepare a place for you? And if I go and
prepare a place for you, I will come again and will
take you to myself, that where I am you may be
also.* (John 14:1-3)

Let me make something clear: I am not a Bible-thumper. I do
not have a bumper sticker which reads, *"Waiting for the Rapture."*
I do not believe, as did my fellow Yale graduate Jonathan Edwards,
that

*... the God that holds you over the pit of hell, much
as one holds a spider or some loathsome insect over
the fire, abhors you, and is dreadfully provoked.
His wrath towards you burns like fire; he looks
upon you as worthy of nothing else but to be cast
into the fire. He is of purer eyes than to bear you in
his sight; you are ten thousand times as abominable
in his eyes as the most hateful, venomous serpent
is in ours.*

Since in this book I have already quoted at length some repugnant political verbiage from my judicial campaigns, let me offer here some repugnant theological verbiage, a bit more of Edwards's 1741 rant. Perhaps Edwards will serve as a cleansing antidote to the political filth I gave you earlier:

> *You have offended him infinitely more than ever a stubborn rebel did his prince, and yet it is nothing but his hand that holds you from falling into the fire every moment.*
>
> *It is to be ascribed to nothing else that you did not go to hell the last night; that you were suffered to awake again in this world, after you closed your eyes to sleep.*
>
> *And there is no other reason to be given why you have not dropped into hell since you arose in the morning, but that God's hand has held you up.*
>
> *There is no other reason to be given why you have not gone to hell since you have sat here in the house of God provoking his pure eye by your sinful, wicked manner of attending his solemn worship.*
>
> *Yea, there is nothing else that is to be given as a reason why you do not this very moment drop down into hell.*
>
> *O sinner! consider the fearful danger you are in! It is a great furnace of wrath, a wide and bottomless pit, full of the fire of wrath that you are held over in the hand of that God whose wrath is provoked and incensed as much against you as against many of the damned in hell.*
>
> *You hang by a slender thread, with the flames of Divine wrath flashing about it, and ready every moment to singe it and burn it asunder. . . .*

There is reason to think that there are many in this congregation, now hearing this discourse, that will actually be the subjects of this very misery to all eternity. We know not who they are, or in what seats they sit, or what thoughts they now have. It may be they are now at ease, and hear all these things without much disturbance, and are now flattering themselves that they are not the persons, promising themselves that they shall escape.

. . . .

And it would be a wonder, if some that are now present should not be in hell in a very short time, before this year is out.

And it would be no wonder if some persons that now sit here in some seats of this meeting-house, in health, and quiet and secure, should be there before tomorrow morning!

Sinners in the Hands of an Angry God

Enfield, Massachusetts

1741

With that then, let us leave Edwards aside. In my opinion we have hope of heaven for more reasons than the New Testament passages above. I am bold to say that those of us who give the matter serious consideration have the sense—the personal, intense knowledge—that it is so.

We know that there is more after this earthly life, and that the particular grandparent and parent await us there. Forget the streets of gold. There will be chocolate donuts in heaven.

Chapter 33

A NEW CHRISTMAS CAROL

My favorite Christmas carol has always been *"Oh, Holy Night."* But last year I encountered the amazing *"Mary, Did You Know?"* (Mark Lowry/Buddy Greene) sung *a cappella* by Pentatonix:

> *Mary, did you know*
> *that your Baby Boy would one day walk on water?*
> *Mary, did you know*
> *that your Baby Boy would save our sons and daughters?*
> *Did you know*
> *that your Baby Boy has come to make you new?*
> *This Child that you delivered will soon deliver you?*
>
> *Mary, did you know*
> *that your Baby Boy will give sight to a blind man?*
> *Mary, did you know*
> *that your Baby Boy will calm the storm with His hand?*
> *Did you know*
> *that your Baby Boy has walked where angels trod?*
> *When you kiss your little Baby you kissed the face of God?*

You may disagree with me, but I find this an astounding change of perspective. A change from, if you will, our own all-centeredness as consumers of Christ's coming (*"Oh come, all ye faithful, joyful and triumphant . . ."*) to Mary's view of the event.

Mary did you know... Ooo Ooo Ooo...
The blind will see.
The deaf will hear.
The dead will live again.
The lame will leap.
The dumb will speak
The praises of The Lamb.

Mary, did you know
that your Baby Boy is Lord of all creation?
Mary, did you know
that your Baby Boy would one day rule the nations?
Did you know
that your Baby Boy is heaven's perfect Lamb?
The sleeping Child you're holding is the Great, I Am.

Yes, she has been through the Annunciation (Luke 1:26) and has spent three months with Elizabeth, who is carrying John the Baptist, but now her own baby boy is here! The one foretold.

What is she thinking? Does she have foreknowledge of what is to come? And if she does, then she sees the crucifixion already, the baby boy in her arms, nailed and dead. It is merciful that the carol does not take us there. But we think of it, of her wonder, of her joy, and of her coming grief.

This carol is not a Catholic veneration-of-Mary argument. It is our song for her, her song, about her foreknowledge perhaps, about her fears or not. About her wonder certainly. But definitely our wonder, our grief, our foreknowledge.

Chapter 34

AN OLD CHRISTMAS CAROL

"*God Rest Ye Merry, Gentlemen*" dates at least to the 16th century. The comma following "merry" is correct. "Merry" is an adverb. The verb "to rest" is used transitively here, an old usage of "rest":

> *God rest ye merry, gentlemen,*
> *Let nothing you dismay.*
> *Remember, Christ, our Saviour*
> *Was born on Christmas day*
> *To save us all from Satan's power*
> *When we were gone astray.*
> *O tidings of comfort and joy,*
> *Comfort and joy,*
> *O tidings of comfort and joy.*

This first stanza is followed by five expository (and not very successful) stanzas, concluding with the seventh stanza (which most of us think of now as the second stanza):

> *Now to the Lord sing praises,*
> *All you within this place,*
> *And with true love and brotherhood*
> *Each other now embrace;*

This holy tide of Christmas
All others doth deface.
O tidings of comfort and joy,
Comfort and joy,
O tidings of comfort and joy.

The carol is referred to, not very accurately, in Dickens's 1843 *Christmas Carol* this way:

> *... at the first sound of 'God bless you, merry gentlemen! May nothing you dismay!', Scrooge seized the ruler with such energy of action that the singer fled in terror, leaving the keyhole to the fog and even more congenial frost.*

Perhaps the change from "rest" to "bless" helps emphasize Scrooge's suspicion of Christmas, religion and all. He certainly does not hear the original wish, that he may rest merry.

Scrooge as we know is anything but merry at this point in his life. Soon it will change:

> *"There's the saucepan that the gruel was in!" cried Scrooge, starting off again, and going round the fireplace. "There's the door, by which the Ghost of Jacob Marley entered! There's the corner where the Ghost of Christmas Present sat! There's the window where I saw the wandering Spirits! It's all right, it's all true, it all happened. Ha ha ha!"*
> *Really, for a man who had been out of practice for so many years, it was a splendid laugh, a most illustrious laugh. The father of a long, long line of brilliant laughs!*

And his joy is our joy, his relief our relief. The grim future he could have lived will not be his. His Christmas leaps up in our hearts. We are glad with him. This marvellous "Ghost Story of Christmas" (the Dickens subtitle) is galloping to a joyous conclusion:

> Running to the window, he opened it, and put out his head. No fog, no mist; clear, bright, jovial, stirring, cold; cold, piping for the blood to dance to; Golden sunlight; Heavenly sky; sweet fresh air; merry bells. Oh, glorious! Glorious!
>
> "What's to-day!" cried Scrooge, calling downward to a boy in Sunday clothes . . .
>
> "Eh?" returned the boy, with all his might of wonder.
>
> "What's to-day, my fine fellow?" said Scrooge.
>
> "To-day!" replied the boy. "Why, Christmas Day."
>
> "It's Christmas Day!" said Scrooge to himself. "I haven't missed it. The Spirits have done it all in one night. They can do anything they like. Of course they can. Of course they can. Hallo, my fine fellow!"
>
> "Hallo!" returned the boy.
>
> "Do you know the Poulterer's, in the next street but one, at the corner?" Scrooge inquired.
>
> "I should hope I did," replied the lad.
>
> "An intelligent boy!" said Scrooge. "A remarkable boy! Do you know whether they've sold the prize Turkey that was hanging up there?—Not the little prize Turkey: the big one?"
>
> "What, the one as big as me?" returned the boy.
>
> "What a delightful boy!" said Scrooge. "It's a pleasure to talk to him. Yes, my buck!"
>
> "It's hanging there now," replied the boy.
>
> "Is it?" said Scrooge. "Go and buy it."
>
> "Walk-er!" exclaimed the boy.

"No, no," said Scrooge, "I am in earnest. Go and buy it, and tell 'em to bring it here, that I may give them the direction where to take it. Come back with the man, and I'll give you a shilling. Come back with him in less than five minutes and I'll give you half-a-crown!"

Scrooge goes to the Cratchits' home, joins in their Christmas dinner, raises Bob's wages the next day, and becomes in all things a merry man:

Scrooge was better than his word. He did it all, and infinitely more; and to Tiny Tim, who did not die, he was a second father. He became as good a friend, as good a master, and as good a man, as the good old city knew, or any other good old city, town, or borough, in the good old world.

Chapter 35

BEULAH LAND

Many are the received phrases of enthusiastic Protestant Christianity—"rock of ages," Beulah land, Calvary, Jordan's shore, pearly gates, streets of gold, washed in the blood, bride of Christ, ebenezer, and many others. To an outsider—or to a skeptic—it must seem overwhelming, a secret fraternity with inside knowledge, code words, strange handshakes. Or maybe the outsider or skeptic just dismisses all the received phrases as embarrassing gobbledygook. Let's take a closer look at some of these words and phrases.

Beulah land

Beulah land is one of the more Delphic terms. I will wager that maybe five percent of Christians know what it is, or purports to be, where it came from. The phrase comes from Isaiah 62:

> *You shall no more be termed Forsaken,*
> *And your land shall no more be termed Desolate,*
> *But you shall be called My Delight is in Her,*
> *And your land Married;*
> *For the Lord delights in you,*
> *And your land shall be married.*

For as a young man marries a young woman,
So shall your sons marry you,
And as the bridegroom rejoices over the bride,
So shall your God rejoice over you.

This is the English Standard Version (ESV) translation. However, in the King James (KJV) translation of Isaiah, the Hebrew people receive not the English phrase, "my delight is in her," but the name *Hephzibah* and their land is married (*Beulah*) to God.

"Beulah" was noticed by John Bunyan, and he decided to use it in his 1678 *Pilgrim's Progress* (in its full title, *The Pilgrim's Progress from This World to That Which Is to Come; Delivered under the Similitude of a Dream.*) Bunyan's work gave Beulah Land the notice and currency it enjoys today.

> *After this, I beheld until they were come unto the Land of Beulah, where the sun shineth night and day. Here, because they were weary, they betook themselves a while to rest; and, because this country was common for pilgrims, and because the orchards and vineyards that were here belonged to the King of the Celestial country, therefore they were licensed to make bold with any of His things. But a little while soon refreshed them here; for the bells did so ring, and the trumpets continually sound so melodiously, that they could not sleep; and yet they received as much refreshing, as if they had slept their sleep ever so soundly.*

For Bunyan's pilgrims, Beulah land is a place from which they can see heaven. It is the last station of good people on the way to heaven.

Beulah land was then incorporated into Southern gospel,

perhaps best by Allison Krauss. Both John Bunyan and our gospel hymns push the idea that heaven can be seen from Beulah land. So Beulah is a good place to which persons yearn to go, in music at least.

The translation of the Bible that King James brought about in 1611—sixty-seven years before Bunyan's *Pilgrim's Progress*—just happened to use the Hebrew word for "married," *Beulah*, instead of good plain English. And thus literature and music were changed.

Rock of ages

There is a hymn which is largely responsible for the vitality of the phrase "rock of ages":

> *Rock of Ages, cleft for me,*
> *Let me hide myself in Thee;*
> *Let the water and the blood,*
> *From Thy riven side which flowed,*
> *Be of sin the double cure,*
> *Cleanse me from its guilt and power.*
>
> *Not the labour of my hands*
> *Can fulfill Thy law's demands;*
> *Could my zeal no respite know,*
> *Could my tears forever flow,*
> *All for sin could not atone;*
> *Thou must save, and Thou alone.*
>
> *Nothing in my hand I bring,*
> *Simply to Thy cross I cling;*
> *Naked, come to Thee for dress;*
> *Helpless, look to Thee for grace;*
> *Foul, I to the fountain fly;*
> *Wash me, Saviour, or I die!*

While I draw this fleeting breath,
When mine eyes shall close in death,
When I soar to worlds unknown,
See Thee on Thy judgement throne,
Rock of Ages, cleft for me,
Let me hide myself in Thee.

The hymn was written in 1763 by minister Augustus Toplady after he was caught in a storm, as the story goes, in the gorge of Burrington Combe in England. The reverend found a gap in the rock wall and took shelter there. The place of shelter has now become a tourist destination and has given its name to a nearby tea shop.

Just as Bunyan was recycling Isaiah's "Beulah," Toplady used Exodus 17: 2-7:

> *. . and the people grumbled against Moses and said, "Why did you bring us up out of Egypt, to kill us and our children and our livestock with thirst?"*
>
> *So Moses cried to the Lord, "What shall I do with this people? They are almost ready to stone me."*
>
> *And the Lord said to Moses, "Pass on before the people, taking with you some of the elders of Israel, and take in your hand the staff with which you struck the Nile, and go. Behold, I will stand before you there on the rock at Horeb, and you shall strike the rock, and water shall come out of it, and the people will drink."*
>
> *And Moses did so, in the sight of the elders of Israel.*

This is seen as a prefiguring of Christ, who was smitten and water flowed from his side, John 19:31-34:

> *Since it was the day of Preparation, and so that the bodies would not remain on the cross on the Sabbath (for that Sabbath was a high day), the Jews asked Pilate that their legs might be broken and that they might be taken away. So the soldiers came and broke the legs of the first, and of the other who had been crucified with him. But when they came to Jesus and saw that he was already dead, they did not break his legs. But one of the soldiers pierced his side with a spear, and at once there came out blood and water.*

But of course there is more going on with "rock of ages" than just a cleavage in a rock wall in England. Both Christ and Peter are firmly associated with rock. "Rock" is Peter's name in Greek, and upon that rock Christ stated he would build his church. But before Peter, Christ was the rock: "The stone which the builders rejected has become the cornerstone" (Psalm 118:22). Or again, in Isaiah 28:16:

> *. . .therefore thus says the Lord God, "Behold, I am the one who has laid as a foundation in Zion, a stone, a tested stone, a precious cornerstone, of a sure foundation: 'Whoever believes will not be in haste.' And I will make justice the line, and righteousness the plumb line; and hail will sweep away the refuge of lies . . ."*

Expanding the metaphor, Paul says in 1 Corinthians 10:1-4:

For I do not want you to be unaware, brothers, that
our fathers were all under the cloud, and all passed
through the sea, and all were baptized into Moses
in the cloud and in the sea, and all ate the same
spiritual food, and all drank the same spiritual
drink. For they drank from the spiritual Rock that
followed them, and the Rock was Christ.

So the scriptural underpinning for "rock of ages" is vast and solid, if mixed, and far more extensive than the one translational reference to Beulah. But it was Augustus Toplady's hymn which made the phrase, "rock of ages" popular.

Calvary

This is the place, or hill, or—as frequently in hymns—"mount" or "mountain," upon which Jesus was crucified. It has nothing to do with military horseback riders ("cavalry"), though I thought so as a child, wondering why some churches had chosen equestrian soldiers as part of their name.

The real explanation is every bit as strange as my cavalry/calvalry confusion. We are told by scholars that a traditional location for crucifixions in Jerusalem was just outside one of the city gates, at a place called *Golgotha* (an Aramaic word meaning "place of the skull"). Scholars have suggested the possibility that the name came from skulls lying around, or that it was a skull-shaped hill where the crucifixions occurred. However, a reliable explanation is not necessary for us because at this point pesky translators stirred the broth.

When producing a Latin text on the death of Jesus in Luke, the King James translators used an anglicised version—*Calvary*—of the Latin from the Vulgate bible (*Calvariæ*), to refer to *Golgotha* in Luke, rather than to translate it. Subsequent uses of *Calvary* simply stem from this single translation decision. The Latin word for "skull" simply replaced *Golgotha*.

The Vulgate version of the bible was largely the work of St. Jerome, who in 382 AD was commissioned by Pope Damasus I to revise the *Vetus Latina* ("Old Latin") collection of biblical texts in Latin then in use by the church. Once published, it was widely adopted and eventually eclipsed the *Vetus Latina*. At the Council of Trent (1545-63 AD) the Catholic Church affirmed the Vulgate version as its official Latin Bible.

If you are a word person, you have to love this little arcane corner of Christian vocabulary development. Christ was crucified on Calvary.

Ebenezer

The Hebrew for "stone of help" is what we are dealing with here. *Ebhen* ("stone") plus *ezer* ("help"). Samuel is responsible:

> *Then Samuel took a stone and set it up between Mizpah and Shen and called its name Ebenezer; for he said, "Till now the Lord has helped us." So the Philistines were subdued and did not again enter the territory of Israel. And the hand of the Lord was against the Philistines all the days of Samuel.*
> *1 Samuel 7:12-13*

LOVE

Chapter 36

EPIPHANY

Epiphany celebrates light. Epiphany celebrates the three wise men bringing gifts to the Christ child. Epiphany celebrates the recognition of light in the world.

Diana, my wonderful wife, was born 6 January, Epiphany Day. The day of the adoration of the Magi. I had no gift for her birthday. So I wrote a poem:

Epiphany, 6 January 2010

I start this poem with "I",
because it is as much about me as it is about you,
even though it is your poem,
your birthday poem.

I start this poem with "I",
because I'm the guy who loves you,
who loves what you do, the one who knows you.

You take care of your mother,
You took care of mine.
You take care of your children,
You take care of mine.

You feed the cat, when she makes you do it.
You do not wash my truck,
at least not yet, but the year is long. One has hope.

I could start this poem with "You",
because it is all about you and not about me at all.
I am the listener in the forest when the tree falls.

I hear my quartermaster stock the larder.
I hear my keeper of linens,
feeder of cardinals, planter of pansies,
purchasing agent, cheese board specialist.

Our home is partly still bedecked for Christmas,
most all the finery in boxes now, and cherished,
to sleep eleven months and reappear.

Soon you'll deck our home for spring,
then summer, fall, and Hallowe'en.
A turkey will come, and paper-whites,
The boxes will reappear, the circle will be whole again.

I will smell your lilies on the hill.
I will gather mums and glads
and bring them to you in my arms.

Another year with you, my dear, is coming.
The Magi are here.
I will eat shepherd's pie, and fish-in-a-pouch,
and sing aloud for the joy of life.

I am the listener in the forest when the tree falls,
I am the listener. The blessings fall around me.
This poem is about you, my dear, just you.
It is yours, all yours. Your birthday poem.

Readers of my first book know the importance of poetry for our marriage. They ask me, "Well, Diana just had a birthday. Did you write her a poem?" I am honored by the question. But, because the poems I write for Diana are so emotional for me, the answer is usually, "No, not this time. But maybe next time."

Chapter 37

NARRATIVE TECHNIQUE, POOH, AND E.T.A. HOFFMANN

As I told you in my second introduction at the start of the book, I love the "how" of storytelling. To be sure, that is a kind of "love," it is an enthusiasm. But it is a technical kind of love. It's what I was looking at in Berlin, 1968-69, finishing my dissertation on E.T.A. Hoffmann's narrative technique. [ENDNOTE 8]

As I write these words, I realize that not just my literacy but also my fascination with the "how" of storytelling began at age four with my mother reading *Winnie the Pooh* to me.

A.A. Milne's narrative presentation is complex and layered. Sometimes it is hard to follow. For example, at the start of the book, Milne formally introduces Edward Bear to the reader, then tells his real son, Christopher Robin, who is listening to the story, how it is that Edward Bear got "Pooh" for a name. He then addresses the reader (us); then he tells Christopher Robin what happened next with Edward Bear; then he gives us Piglet's fears, Eeyore's grumpy ruminations, Owl's frantic obfuscations, and on and on through the many adventures.

It ends in the tenth chapter, "In Which Christopher Robin Gives A Pooh Party, And We Say Good-bye." Pooh receives a pencil box at the party. (Christopher Robin, in the other plane, the real plane, the son of the author, is preparing for school.) Pooh's exploratory joy with his pencil box is Milne's vehicle to explain to Christopher Robin, his son, his own pencil box:

> *It was a Special Pencil Case. There were pencils in it marked B" for Bear, and pencils marked "HB" for Helping Bear, and pencils marked "BB" for Brave Bear. There was a knife for sharpening the pencils, and india-rubber for rubbing out anything which you had spelt wrong, and a ruler for ruling lines for the words to walk on, and inches marked on the ruler in case you wanted to know how many inches anything was, and Blue Pencils and Red Pencils and Green Pencils for saying special things in blue and red and green. And all these lovely things were in little pockets of their own in a Special Case which shut with a click when you clicked it. And they were all for Pooh.*
> *"Oh!" said Pooh.*
> *"Oh, Pooh!" said everybody else except Eeyore.*
> *"Thank-you," growled Pooh.*
> *But Eeyore was saying to himself, "This writing business. Pencils and what-not. Over-rated, if you ask me. Silly stuff. Nothing in it."*

This is the end of the first book. As if the complexity developed so far were not enough, it deepens with the introduction to the second book, *The House at Pooh Corner:*

Contradiction

> *An Introduction is to introduce people, but Christopher Robin and his friends, who have already been introduced to you, are now going*

*to say Good-bye. So this is the opposite . . . Owl
kept his head and told us that the opposite of an
Introduction, my dear Pooh, was a Contradiction;
and, as he is very good at long words, I am sure that
that's what it is. Why we are having a Contradiction
is because last week when Christopher Robin said
to me, "What about that story you were going to
tell me about what happened to Pooh when—" I
happened to say very quickly, "What about nine
times a hundred and seven?" And when we had
done that one, we had one about cows going
through a gate at two a minute, and there are three
hundred in the field, so how many are left after an
hour and a half?*

This is complex storytelling. Our minds are swimming.

My dissertation centered on one particular corner of storytelling and on one particular author: how Ernst Theodor Amadeus Hoffmann (1776- 1822) presents the fantastic elements in his fiction.

In 1816 Hoffmann wrote *Nutcracker and Mouse King* (*Nussknacker und Mäusekönig*). This one story is all most Americans know about Hoffman, and that little bit we usually get only from Tchaikovsky's 1892 Christmas ballet, *The Nutcracker.*

Hoffmann wrote many stories, many set outside the normal planes of reality. He was writing midway in German Romanticism, hard on the heels of the rational, austere, scientific world of the Enlightenment. In comparison with English Romanticism, the German variety of Romanticism developed late, and in its early years coincided with so-called Weimar Classicism, which ran from 1772 to 1805. It is fair to say that in contrast to the seriousness of English Romanticism, the German variety valued wit, humour, and beauty.

How was Hoffmann to get away with his breaks from rational

reality? How could he present his irrational stories without offending his rational readers? His answer was to cheat.

Hoffmann "softened" his stories—a term I introduced to literary criticism—by giving his readers various safety nets to prevent them from falling headlong fall into fantasia. Stephen King does not soften the irrational. Nora Roberts in her Irish trilogies does not soften.

Washington Irving does. Think of the safety net in Irving's "*The Legend of Sleepy Hollow*": Perhaps Ichabod Crane has simply disappeared, Irving suggests, frightened away by his rival, Brom Bones, and is now practicing law in a distant part of New York state. True, there is a pumpkin head smashed in the road, but . . . On the other hand, in Tim Burton's 1999 film *Sleepy Hollow*, we see a real headless horseman many times. There is no apology for, or softening of, the rampant magic.

Let me be professorial for a moment: Behind every story, every novel, every film, there is a governing intelligence directing your journey. You will sense her governing intelligence clearly, for example, in the opening lines of Jane Austen's *Pride and Prejudice*, a gently sarcastic social observer:

> *It is a truth universally acknowledged, that a single man in possession of a good fortune, must be in want of a wife. However little known the feelings or views of such a man may be on his first entering a neighbourhood, this truth is so well fixed in the minds of the surrounding families, that he is considered the rightful property of some one or other of their daughters.*

This governing intelligence is called a "persona." You will either like the persona directing your journey or you will not. She/he may be meticulously unobtrusive, and if so you will have no opinion of him; you will be largely unaware of your tour guide.

The point is, he is there, a guiding intelligence. Jane Austen's persona is obvious throughout the novel.

With Hoffmann, the tour guide is predisposed to accepting the wondrous. He is intrigued with mystery. However, he is careful not to offend his gentle reader with unabashedly preposterous things. He does not say, as Nora Roberts does, "Fairies are real. Get ready for a story about fairies." You trust Hoffmann's persona: Hoffmann makes clear the adventures Marie and Fritz have in *Nussknacker und Mäusekönig* may well have been nothing more than a dream.

But think of *"The Cremation of Sam McGee"* by Robert Service, the stuff of many a Hallowe'en recital. Here we move from the coldly rational, nights-long dogsled trip (the real world), corpse lashed fast to the sled,

> *Now a promise made is a debt unpaid,*
> *and the trail has its own stern code.*
> *In the days to come, though my lips were dumb,*
> *in my heart how I cursed that load.*
> *In the long, long night, by the lone firelight,*
> *while the huskies, round in a ring,*
> *Howled out their woes to the homeless snows —*
> *O God! how I loathed the thing.*

to the ice-bound ship whose furnace will be the crematorium. But it is still very much a part of the rational world:

> *Some planks I tore from the cabin floor,*
> *and I lit the boiler fire;*
> *Some coal I found that was lying around,*
> *and I heaped the fuel higher;*
> *The flames just soared, and the furnace roared —*
> *such a blaze you seldom see;*
> *And I burrowed a hole in the glowing coal,*

and I stuffed in Sam McGee.
Then I made a hike, for I didn't like to hear him
sizzle so;
And the heavens scowled, and the huskies howled,
and the wind began to blow.
It was icy cold, but the hot sweat rolled
down my cheeks, and I don't know why;
And the greasy smoke in an inky cloak
went streaking down the sky.
I do not know how long in the snow
I wrestled with grisly fear;
But the stars came out and they danced about
ere again I ventured near;
I was sick with dread, but I bravely said:
"I'll just take a peep inside. I guess he's cooked,
and it's time I looked"; then the door I opened wide.

So far so good. But then Robert Service hits us with the roaring impossibility:

And there sat Sam, looking cool and calm,
in the heart of the furnace roar;
And he wore a smile you could see a mile,
and he said: "Please close that door.
It's fine in here, but I greatly fear
you'll let in the cold and storm —
Since I left Plumtree, down in Tennessee,
it's the first time I've been warm."

This is a headlong fall into the preposterous. Not Hoffmann's style, not Washington Irving's.

On the other hand, Robert Service's persona can sometimes be firmly planted in earthbound boots, as it is in "The Shooting of Dan McGrew":

A bunch of the boys were whooping it up in the Malamute saloon;
The kid that handles the music-box was hitting a jag-time tune;
Back of the bar, in a solo game, sat Dangerous Dan McGrew,
And watching his luck was his light-o'-love, the lady that's known as Lou.
When out of the night, which was fifty below, and into the din and the glare,
There stumbled a miner fresh from the creeks, dog-dirty, and loaded for bear.
He looked like a man with a foot in the grave and scarcely the strength of a louse,
Yet he tilted a poke of dust on the bar, and he called for drinks for the house.

This is a persona who likes honky-tonks, who may not be our cup of tea, but he is completely rational:

I'm not so wise as the lawyer guys, but strictly between us two,
The woman that kissed him—and pinched his poke—
Was the lady that's known as Lou.

In Algernon Blackwood's 1910 "Wendigo," we are back in Hoffmann territory. We readers cannot parse out exactly what has happened in the Canadian woods. (*Maybe Ichabod Crane is practicing law in upstate New York . . .*) Dr. Cathcart posits hallucination, or perhaps that young Simpson is a victim of "auto suggestion." But it is an inescapable narrative fact that Défago fled the tent, disappeared leaving odd tracks, and reappeared miles away, demented and raving:

The details of how he survived the prolonged exposure, of where he had been, or of how he covered the great distance from one camp to the other, including an immense detour of the lake on foot since he had no canoe—all this remains unknown. His memory had vanished completely.

And before the end of the winter whose beginning witnessed this strange occurrence, Défago, bereft of mind, memory and soul, had gone with it. He lingered only a few weeks.

And what Punk was able to contribute to the story throws no further light upon it. He was cleaning fish by the lake shore about five o'clock in the evening—an hour, that is, before the search party returned—when he saw this shadow of the guide picking its way weakly into camp. In advance of him, he declares, came the faint whiff of a certain singular odour.

That same instant old Punk started for home. He covered the entire journey of three days as only Indian blood could have covered it. The terror of a whole race drove him. He knew what it all meant. Défago had "seen the Wendigo."

So what really did happen? Blackwood leaves us in the dark:

With his uncle [Cathcart] he [Simpson] never discussed the matter in detail, for the barrier between the two types of mind made it difficult. Only once, years later, something led them to the frontier of the subject—of a single detail of the subject, rather—

"Can't you even tell me what—they [Défago's feet] were like?" he asked; and the reply, though

conceived in wisdom, was not encouraging, "It is
far better you should not try to know, or to find
out." "Well—that odour...?" persisted the nephew.
"What do you make of that?"
Dr. Cathcart looked at him and raised his eyebrows.
"Odours," he replied, "are not so easy as sounds
and sights of telepathic communication. I make
as much, or as little, probably, as you do yourself."
He was not quite so glib as usual with his
explanations. That was all.

Algernon Blackwood has created a persona who is fully content to leave us confused, a persona who is open to the wondrous, but not completely sure of it. An English Hoffmann.

Chapter 38

GOSPEL MUSIC PART ONE

As you know by now, one of my loves is gospel music. I urge upon you this my opinion: Gospel music can be astounding, as fine and as rich as Mozart, as moving as any Christmas carol.

Oh, I know it is fashionable for intelligentsia to sniff at gospel music, and at country music in general. But am I speaking seriously? That gospel can be as fine as Mozart? Yes, seriously. There is as much majesty in the singing of Jamie Dailey and Darrin Vincent as there is in *The Magic Flute*, Mozart's finest opera. Or in the greatest grandeur of the best Wagnerian operas.

But let's be honest: Gospel music often is not excellent. It can be fatuous, saccharine, embarrassing, and as shallow as a greasy frying pan. How can this be? Well, there's also some bad opera. And opera—we are told—is an elegant art form. (Remember, Antony told us, "Brutus is an honorable man.")

Apparently it makes no difference whether you are worshipping God or art. Either can be done badly. No one sets out to create bad gospel. No one sets out to create bad opera. It just happens.

To plumb the dregs of gospel, you don't have to seek out the frequently poor singing, or look for poor arrangements. But in the bad songs you will often notice poorly chosen words. (Let's be fair: There are tropes, some of them unavoidable, and the vocabulary of Appalachian Christianity is intrinsically limited. But within those confines there can be brilliance, majesty, messages of redemption and hope.)

What I am saying is this: It is not enough to roll out church phrases, however well-intentioned, make them rhyme in three-quarters time, and figure you've done enough. If fine gospel text is a superhighway of piety and devotion, poor gospel is a potholed road of rhyming words flaccid from overuse. The superhighway is Dailey and Vincent, as I said above in the section on faith:

> *When I cross over*
> *I will shout and sing.*
> *I will know my savior*
> *By the mark where the*
> *Nails have been . . .*
> —*Gillian Welch, 1996, Revival*

The best gospel <u>sound</u> in my opinion is produced *a cappella*, with two or more voices, frequently with four. Think of The Wailin' Jennys in "Bright Morning Stars." Rhonda Vincent has a stunning *a cappella* performance of the traditional *"Fishers of Men"*:

> *Peter, John, and James*
> *Could never be the same*
> *After they heard him say*
> *I'll make you fishers of men.*
>
> *Cast your nets aside*
> *and join the battle tide.*
> *He will be your guide*
> *To make you fishers of men.*
>
> *Jesus bore the cross*
> *To gather in the lost.*

Oh what a mighty cost
To set us free from sin.

He said, Rise and follow me,
I'll make you worthy.
Rise and follow me,
I'll make you fishers of men.

A welcome newcomer is Patti Casey, who in 2005 gave us her astounding *a cappella*, *"It All Comes Down"*:

From the time that you set foot upon this earth to
pass your days
You are walking on borrowed ground, and you may
stake no claims
To the soil and to the water, to the creatures lying by.
Even the breath you take is loaned from on high.

It all comes down in the end, all the works of your
hand,
Though built of stone. And honestly no earthly
house shall ever stand.
And it all comes down, down in the end like a hand
full of sand.
And it all comes down, and it all comes down,
down in the end.

As you walk along those borders with the deed held
in your hand,
Just remember you don't own this, you are a
steward of this land.
So seek wisdom and show mercy, leaving some for
another day,
For you will call upon yourself the same someday.

When you drift down like a leaf to find your final
resting place,
You will return what you have borrowed, you will
have to show your face.
And did you help some troubled soul, did you try
to lend a hand?
For only kindness in the end alone shall stand.
                    —Patti Casey, 2005, The Edge of Grace

Dailey and Vincent have an ethereal blend of voices. It is Appalachian plainchant. You will be amazed by their rendering of the traditional *"Farther Along We'll Understand Why"*. A Christian does not miss those references to Ecclesiastes:

> *Tempted and tried we're oft made to wonder*
> *Why it should be thus all the day long,*
> *While there are others living about us*
> *Never molested though in the wrong.*

> *When death has come and taken our loved ones,*
> *It leaves our home so lonely and drear.*
> *And then do we wonder why others prosper,*
> *Living so wicked year after year.*

> *Farther along we'll know all about it.*
> *Farther along we'll understand why.*
> *Cheer up my brother, live in the sunshine.*
> *We'll understand it all by and by.*
> *Yeah, we'll understand it all by and by.*
>   Public domain, W.B. Stevens, 1911

Not *a cappella*, but the absolute showstopper for soprano gospel—are we surprised?—is Dolly Parton, on her *Little Sparrow* album, *"In the Sweet By and By,"*

There's a land that is fairer than day,
And by faith we can see it afar;
For the Father waits over the way
To prepare us a dwelling place there.

> *In the sweet by and by,*
> *We shall meet on that beautiful shore;*
> *In the sweet by and by,*
> *We shall meet on that beautiful shore.*

We shall sing on that beautiful shore
The melodious songs of the blessed;
And our spirits shall sorrow no more,
Not a sigh for the blessing of rest.

To our bountiful Father above,
We will offer our tribute of praise
For the glorious gift of His love
And the blessings that hallow our days.

Sanford F. Bennett, 1868
Public domain

Excellent *a cappella* is Dailey and Vincent's take on Jimmy Fortune's song, a telling of the parable of the prodigal son (Luke 15:11). If you can listen to this performance and not weep, you are stronger than I:

> *I was once a wayward child,*
> *Thought I had all the answers.*
> *Foolish heart and foolish dreams,*
> *The world was my master.*
>
> *I found myself a broken man*
> *In need of love and compassion.*

And the words of my father
Came back to me.

"Come back to me my child
For my arms are open wide.
Come back to me and rest in my love.
I'll never turn away
No matter how lost you may be.
You can always come back to me."

As I made my way back home
I couldn't help but wonder
Would he even know my name?
Would he still keep his promise?
Ashamed of everything I've done,
Would he ever forgive me?
And the words of my father
Came back to me:

"Come back to me my child
For my arms are open wide.
Come back to me and rest in my love.
I'll never turn away
No matter how lost you may be.
You can always come back to me."

And I stood on that hill,
I looked at my home.
Tears filled my eyes,
And I felt so alone.
Then I saw my father come running to me,
His arms stretched out.
I fell on my knees,
Oh, I fell on my knees.

He said, "I love you, son.
I'm so glad you've come back to me."

This of course is the "joy in heaven" from Luke 15, that chapter which gives us three parables back-to-back: the prodigal son, the lost sheep, the lost coin.

"Just so, I tell you, there will be more joy in heaven
over one sinner who repents than over ninety-nine
righteous persons who need no repentance."

If you doubt whether God loves you, go to Luke 15.

As for more *a capella*, absolutely excellent is Blue Highway's *"Chasing Down the Wind,"* in a minor key, and their joyous *"I'm Near the Gate,"* and *"What Wondrous Love Is This?"* Other great *a capella* performances are by Joe Mullins and the Radio Ramblers, *"Rock of Ages Keep My Soul," "Set My People Free"*; and David Parmley & Continental Divide, *"I'll Be A Friend to Jesus"*. On an album called *Hymns and Songs of the Mormon Pioneers*, Lisa Arrington has a remarkable *a cappella* rendering of *"Come Thou Font of Every Blessing."*

Perhaps the best *a cappella* gospel hymn of all is done by Russell Moore and IIIrd Tyme Out performing *"Swing Low Sweet Chariot."*

Do not miss Dailey and Vincent's tour de force, *"Don't You Want to Go To Heaven?"* but most particularly do not miss their close harmony in *"When I've Traveled My Last Mile."* Here there is a light instrumental accompaniment to a chilling duet descant.

Second tenors

You don't have to sing *a cappella* to create great gospel sound. Paul Williams is a rich solo second tenor who, lacking the Nashville reverb, is simple, plain, straightforward, and excellent.

"I Went Down A Beggar," or *"I'll Be Young Again When I Get Over There"*:

> *You know sometimes my hands are not so steady,*
> *And I know my steps are slow and there's silver in*
> *my hair.*
> *But I'm as happy as I can be because I know what's*
> *waiting for me.*
> *I'll be young again when I get over there.*
> > -Paul Williams and The Victory Trio, What A
> > Journey

There are other great second tenors, Cody Shuler of Pine Mountain Railroad, covering the oft-recorded hymn, *"Where the Soul of a Man Never Dies"*:

> *To Canaan's land I'm on my way,*
> *Where the soul of a man never dies;*
> *My darkest night will turn to day,*
> *Where the soul never dies.*
> > William Matthew Golden, copyright 1914, First
> > published 1915,
> > *Calvary Hymns*, Ft. Worth, TX

Or again, the fine second tenor Don Rigsby in *"Drifting Too Far From the Shore,"* an old song recorded by everyone from Hank Williams Sr. to Bill Monroe and Emmylou Harris:

> *Out on the perilous deep*
> *Where dangers silently creep*
> *And storms so violently sweep*
> *You're drifting too far from the shore.*
> *Drifting too far from the shore (from the shore)*
> *Drifting too far from the shore (peaceful shore)—*
> *Come to Jesus today, let him show you the way.*

You're drifting too far from the shore.

Charles Ernest Moody, 1923,
Dalton, GA

Chapter 39

GOSPEL MUSIC PART TWO

The worst gospel sound, when it occurs, is a cacophony of mediocre voices, frequently with one rickety piano or other poor accompaniment: The Kentucky Colonels (*"Over in the Glory Land"*).

In between the best and the worst sounds there is the sincere, invasive, studio-produced second tenor—some pompous Bing Crosby of Christianity—who sings slowly and sincerely about God. It will have heavy accompaniment, and a thick, textured, round, "You-are-there-in-the-Nashville-sound-studio," feel.

As Abraham Lincoln is thought to have said, "People who like this sort of thing will find this the sort of thing they like." There are many who do like it. I am not one. See examples with Alan Jackson, *"How Great Thou Art"*, or Don Edwards, *"I Saw the Light."*

In my middle group of second tenors is Johnny Cash, who is a bass, not a second tenor, and is in my opinion head and shoulders above Alan Jackson.

The opposite extreme in sound is the casual chaos of the Stanley Brothers (or Ralph Stanley and others after Carter Stanley died in 1966 of alcoholism)—brilliant gospel, usually a duo, frequently tonally flat, riding on excellent banjo, mandolin and flat-top. All acoustic, of course. Ralph Stanley also owns the best cover of Dick Burnett's 1913, *"I Am A Man of Constant Sorrow,"* arranged by brother Carter:

> *Maybe your friends think I'm just a stranger.*
> *My face you never will see no more.*
> *But there is one promise that is given—*
> *I'll meet you on God's golden shore.*

If you tone down the chaos of Ralph Stanley, you get the discipline of Doyle Lawson and Quicksilver: solid, almost mechanical mandolin and banjo with competent voices. But the sound is frequently only almost just good enough. So after a while you stop listening to Doyle Lawson and Quicksilver, and go back to Ralph Stanley or Boxcar Willie.

For outstanding soprano sound, look no further than Alison Krauss in *"A Living Prayer,"* or Patty Loveless with Ricky Skaggs in *"Daniel Prayed,"* or Orla Fallon in *"Down to the River to Pray."*

There is outstanding instrumental-only gospel music: Marc Burchfield performing *"Leaning on Everlasting Arms."*

Spoiler alert: no credible gospel can be done with dobro guitar or electric organ. Example: Guy Penrod, solid second tenor, *"The Old Rugged Cross"*: Over-produced, heavy, breathy Nashville studio sound, and worst of all, dobro.

Chapter 40

STRUNK AND WHITE
MEET THE MAILBOX

Here is another of my loves: language. This is a strong love. Oh, not as strong as my love for Diana, but deeply and abidingly strong. My eleven law clerks know its strength.

Winnie the Pooh, a little book, and Strunk and White's *Elements of Style,* another little book, are the cornerstones of my literacy.

Strunk and White tell us, *"Form the possessive singular of nouns by adding 's. Follow this rule whatever the final consonant."* And so, they instruct us, *"Thus write: Charles's friend, Burns's poems, the witch's malice."*

Simple and straightforward, these rules. There are exceptions for *"ancient proper names ending in -es and -is, the possessive Jesus', and such forms as for conscience' sake, for righteousness' sake."*

All of us who write English know that plurals are formed by adding an "s"—unless the final letter is already an "s" or is a sibilant. Then we add "es". So we have bosses, horses, fishes, and witches. That's it for plurals, except for some special words which change their stem vowels: Goose becomes geese. Mouse becomes mice. Oh, and then those words which are both singular and plural, like deer, moose, and counsel (lawyer/lawyers).

But possessives—the apostrophes of which Strunk and White speak—have absolutely nothing do with forming plurals. We know this. Absolutely nothing. This is without doubt. End of discussion.

Except in my hometown of Knoxville, where mailboxes tell us the contrary. See for example the mailbox in front of the Herbert home. It firmly proclaims: "The Herbert's."

I look forward to meeting this fellow, "The Herbert." He must be exceptional. Or perhaps the message means that the mailbox, the house, and the land all belong to "The Herbert." That these things are all possessed by him.

Apparently, this fellow, "The Herbert," lives alone, as befits his uniqueness. Perhaps he has an Indian blanket and is himself the stuff of legend. If the monster Grendel from *Beowulf* should encounter "The Herbert," who would win?

In my mother's hometown of Hancock, Maine, population 600 [ENDNOTE 7], the Murphys (not the Murphy's) defined and ruined welfare. The town formally made note in town meeting of the Murphys' (or is it the Murphy's's?) poverty, and voted them town wood. Various men from the town delivered the wood a cord at a time through the winter. On the coast of Maine a family of six can, in a hard winter, burn four cords of wood. In their second winter of town wood, the Murphys took delivery of ten cords. They sold the extra six.

The Murphys did not engage in crony capitalism. They never had the opportunity. They would have, if they could have.

Chapter 41

TEACH YOUR CHILDREN ENGLISH

<u>Is</u> breathing a skill? No, but it is necessary to life. I believe that the effective and precise use of English is necessary to life. Notice, please, that I did not say "proper" English—although that brings advantages you will explain to your children.

But you definitely do not want to raise them to be language snobs. While I can speak "proper" English, indeed I have to do so to earn a living—the practice of law requires it—I can also speak East Tennessee, and usually do.

You will teach your children that we would all still be speaking Latin now, if language were not a continually evolving and changing ocean of sound. For an example your children can understand, tell them that "text" was never, ever, ever a verb. That is, until the 21st century. They probably won't believe you.

Then tell them that until the 21st century "impact" was always a noun. Tell them that for language purists, "text" and "impact" will always be nouns and will never be verbs, but that we purists are being swept away by the ever-present tide of linguistic creativity.

The very same tide which made "text" and "impact" into verbs made Latin into a new language, in fact, several new languages. The Latin-speaking purists of the fourth century were swept away by their beloved Latin evolving out from under them. They were probably upset. But, too bad, they lost. Now we have Italian, and Spanish, and French, and Romanian, and Portuguese, and English. And no Latin, except snippets in the practice of law, and of course church Latin, which is effectively museum Latin.

Teach your children about cultural islands of older locutions. "Poke sallet." "I come home yestiddy." "I done done it." Teach them about accents. Teach them that the possessive singular is always formed by adding an apostrophe plus an "s": The fish's belly. Gilbert's pencil. Charles's friend. That the only exception is "its," which does in fact mean "possessed by the it." As in, "Its handle is broken." Teach them that "it's" is a contraction for, and means, "it is." As in, "It's too bad its handle is broken."

Teach them to avoid crude words, and to avoid crude speech in general. It is not, as some think, a useful ploy for ingratiating yourself with others. It is always a lowering of self. Gross language does not advance discourse. It degrades the speaker.

Teach them that the entire edifice of Western civilization is based on

- Abraham
- Moses,
- Christ,
- Willis Carrier, and
- Strunk & White's *Elements of Style*.
- Oh, yes, and football.

You can jump-start your children's language skills, as my mother did for me, by reading them *Winnie The Pooh* every day. I mean the original 1926 A.A. Milne *Winnie The Pooh*. And then later, if you like, the 1928 sequel, *The House at Pooh Corner*. Only those two Pooh books for language skill and delight. No Disney, not for language skills, not for complex psychology.

If you read your children only one real A.A. Milne *Pooh* story a day for six years, they will be grounded in English and completely sold on its benefits for life.

Chapter 42

FIFTEEN YEARS MARRIED

I had no Hallmark card for our anniversary, no fine storebought expression of my gratitude for fifteen years of marriage to the best wife in the world. So I wrote a poem.

A POEM FOR DIANA
17 November 2012

Fifteen years now.
A wonderful time, brief as a moment, as glorious as sunrise.
Each day the light comes back to our portion of earth.
You awake and smile and the day begins.
Fifteen years now the sun has risen,
making our portion of earth warm, well tended.
The crystal anniversary.
Sunlight fractionated through Waterford glass.
Laughter, love, light, the bevels of our crystal,
a sparkling toast lifted to you.

Chapter 43

AN UNBROKEN LINE OF
GREAT TEACHERS

I can still remember the wonder with which Jerome Taylor and I grasped that you could say something some other way than in English. A completely different set of sounds and symbols. A second language. We were amazed. An utterly new idea. It was a transforming moment, September 1956, ninth grade, the first week of Mr. Webb's Latin class and our first week at Webb School [ENDNOTE 8].

There were a lot of those transforming moments in my four years at Webb. Some of them were "Aha!" moments, like that first encounter with a foreign language, an alternate language. Some of them were "fill-the-backpack" moments—times you knew you were loading up with information you would always need and always use. Some of them were "character" moments— times when I was a good citizen or a poor citizen and learned the consequences.

There were sixteen of us who graduated four years later in the class of 1960. I can name them all, fondly and with pride: "E.B." Boles, Jim Bradley, Sam Colville, David Creekmore, Kit Ewing, Hugh Faust, Jeff Goodson, LeClair Greenblatt, Jim Hart, Peter

Krapf, Ed McCampbell, Doug Newton, Chip Osborn, Sterling Shuttleworth, Clark Smeltzer, and me.

I remember them fondly because of the friendships, successes, embarrassments, mistakes, follies, and secrets; and with pride because of our progress in four years toward a Webb-shaped maturity. There were also moments of grace: Jeff Goodson teaching me to tie a bow tie—it took him three days, but it stuck; Sam Colville teaching me to drive straight shift in his creampuff yellow and white '55 Chevy.

For me and for many of us, there is no "Robert Webb," no "Bob Webb." There is only the great and fine man we called and always will call "Mr. Webb." He came into our lives in the basement of Sequoyah Hills Presbyterian church and changed each one of us forever.

In my life, and I hope in yours, there is an unbroken line of great teachers. For me the line is Miss Freeman, who taught me seventh grade English at Tyson Junior High; Mr. Webb, who introduced me to Latin in the ninth grade; Ted Bruning, my English teacher for four years at Webb; B.E. Sharp, Webb's teacher of life skills; and John Sobieski, professor of Civil Procedure at UT Law School.

The line is unbroken, not because these individuals are all still alive—Miss Freeman, Mr. Webb, and Coach Sharp are physically gone—but because they are all still with me. They always will be. They live in in my house. They are with me when I talk to my children; they are with me when I reach out to others. These five fine people required hard work and excellence in their own lives, and expected the same of me.

I had some good teachers at Harvard and Yale. But I had my great teachers, my five great teachers, in Knoxville. I don't know what that says about education. Perhaps that the best teaching is done by those who are not overly impressed with themselves; by those who love learning and want you to share that love.

Henry Brooks Adams, the great-grandson of John Adams,

said, "A teacher affects eternity; he can never tell where his influence stops." Mr. Webb affected our eternities. He trained us to excellence. Mr. Webb wanted the best from each of us, there in the basement of the church. We delivered him our best because of his enthusiasm for learning. We also delivered him our best because of his evident joy in the life of the mind. We lastly delivered him our best because of his love of life itself.

He wanted us to be leaders. We became leaders, because we wanted to be like him. He took mere human beings and produced leaders: *Principes non homines*, the Latin in his coat of arms.

Chapter 44

SOME PARTING THOUGHTS ON LANGUAGE

It just happened to be Mr. Webb and Latin in the fall of 1956, but it could have been any language. But there it was in print, in a book I owned, right there, something strange, marching along and saying things, and it wasn't saying them in English.

I suspect that when Isaac Newton discovered gravity, he smacked himself on the forehead and said, "Well, of course!" But he was still amazed.

I was certainly amazed. I know that not everyone feels amazement upon encountering a second way of saying something. Not everyone is built to feel the thrill of a new and unknown land. This is because every brain is unique, and some brains just don't want to go exploring *terram novam*. In fact some brains really cannot.

So that means all our serious, well-intentioned efforts to have children learn French or Spanish or Latin will fail with some children, and that the failure will leave those children feeling bad about themselves. And parents feeling bad about their children. Which is wrong for both parents and children.

Perhaps somewhere there is an excellent diagnostic tool to measure language openness in youngsters. If it exists, it should be used to find those children who are not open to foreign languages, and then spare them and their parents years of misery and self-reproach. Best of all, this diagnostic tool would grant the children months and years of freedom, making all that time available to further the skills the children are good at.

But for those children and adults who happen to be comfortable with the symbols and sounds of new lands, there is great fun ahead:

- *perspectives on the homeland of English;*
- *the joys of etymology;*
- *a grasp of the evolution of language;*
- *the fun of cognates;*
- *Chaucer and Beowulf.*

(Of course, it must be confessed that if the second language learned is a Romance language, *Beowulf* remains hopelessly inscrutable. On the other hand, if the second language is a Germanic one, *Beowulf* opens itself.)

Facility for language in general

The joys of Shakespearean English require no second language, only a delight in the intricacy of words. If you delight in word derivation, you have no trouble with "Zounds," "prithee," and "o'erhanging": "Zounds" yields itself to "God's wounds," an exclamation. "Prithee" yields itself to "pray thee," that is, "I request/pray that you do something for me." Someone who can puzzle out "o'erhanging"—

> . . . *look you, this brave o'erhanging firmament,*
> *this majestical roof fretted with golden fire—why,*
> *it appears no other thing to me than a foul and*
> *pestilent congregation of vapors.*
> —*Hamlet, Act II, Scene 2*

can do so because he/she has the facility to see "over" in "o'er," and the flexibility of thought to accept the notion that the sky is "hanging" above, and that the sky might have frets like a mandolin. Or perhaps that the sky is loaded—"fraught"—with golden fire, or has the "freight" of golden fire. That same person has no difficulty delighting in, and remembering forever, that "goodbye" comes from "God be with ye." It is language facility, not acquaintance with a second language, which makes all this possible.

What of Lady Macbeth's words in Act I, Scene V? How difficult is it for a person who enjoys language?

> The raven himself is hoarse
> That croaks the fatal entrance of Duncan
> Under my battlements. Come, you spirits
> That tend on mortal thoughts, unsex me here,
> And fill me, from the crown to the toe, top-full
> Of direst cruelty! Make thick my blood;
> Stop up th' access and passage to remorse,
> That no compunctious visiting of nature
> Shake my fell purpose nor keep peace between
> Th' effect and it! Come to my woman's breasts
> And take my milk for gall, you murth'ring ministers,
> Wherever in your sightless substances
> You wait on nature's mischief! Come, thick night,
> And pall thee in the dunnest smoke of hell,
> That my keen knife see not the wound it makes,
> Nor heaven peep through the blanket of the dark
> To cry 'Hold, hold!'

With "fatal" and "mortal," it is simply facility with language which helps the reader, not a knowledge of some foreign language. "Fatal" is understood outside its basic adjectival meaning of "killing," or "deadly," to also mean "fated" (that is, fated to happen by the three witches). "Mortal" is understood to mean more than "the thoughts of mortals," but additionally "deadly," and "murderous."

"Direst" poses no difficulty in yielding up "most dire." It is an unusual superlative, but the flexible mind accommodates it.

More difficult is the language following "Stop up th' access . . ." But a person who welcomes language can parse it out as a command to the spirits of death to come to Lady Macbeth and block the (imagined) biological duct which might make her feel remorse. She does not want any fussy ("compunctious," "filled with compunction") impulse ("visiting of nature") to interrupt ("shake") her resolve.

"Fell purpose" can't be good, the reader senses, and hears with "fell" the echo of "to fell" a tree, or even "foul." Or the reader might know the ancient meaning of "skin" or "pelt"—hence, "animalistic, primitive." The clause finishes with the wish that no hesitation "make peace" (come between) the outcome (death of Duncan) and the intent to kill him ("fell purpose").

Not easy stuff, that. The rest of the passage is easy: "Murth'ring" is clearly "murdering." "Sightless" has the more obscure meaning of "invisible." "Pall" is here a verb, "to wrap" with cloth, as in the pall of death ("pall bearer"). "Dunnest" is a superlative for "brown."

But once again, let me emphasize that your ability to figure out the Shakespeare has nothing to do with whether or not you have command of a second language. It comes simply because you like language, it is one of your loves, and that makes you good at unraveling the Shakespeare.

Language changes over time

If you are a "language person" you delight in the evolution of English. You know that Chaucer goes on to become Spenser, Spenser goes on to become Shakespeare, Shakespeare goes on to become Poe, and Poe goes on to become Billy Joel.

Let's look at some Chaucer, from *The Canterbury Tales*, written 1387 to 1400 in Middle English:

> **Now telleth ye, sir Monk, if that ye konne,**
> *Now tell you, sir Monk, if you can,*
> **Somwhat to quite with the Knyghtes tale."**
> *Something to equal the Knight's tale."*
> **The Millere, that for dronken was al pale,**
> *The Miller, who for drunkenness was all pale,*
> **So that unnethe upon his hors he sat,**
> *So that he hardly sat upon his horse,*
> **He nolde avalen neither hood ne hat,**
> *He would not doff neither hood nor hat,*
> **Ne abyde no man for his curteisie,**
> *Nor give preference to any man out of courtesy,*
> **But in Pilates voys he gan to crie,**
> *But in Pilate's voice he began to cry,*
> **And swoor, "By armes, and by blood and bones,**
> *And swore, "By (Christ's) arms, and by blood and bones,*
> **I kan a noble tale for the nones,**
> *I know a noble tale for this occasion,*
> **With which I wol now quite the Knyghtes tale."**
> *With which I will now requite the Knight's tale."*
> *The Miller's Tale*

This bit of Middle English is difficult, but it is not hopelessly remote to a language person. Yes, this is our language. Yes, it is hard, but it is not impossible. For example, the next to last line has "kan," which the reader might know is the Scottish "ken," to know, to recognize. As in the song,

> *Do ye ken John Peel with his coat so gay?*
> *Do ye ken John Peel at the break of day?*

Do ye ken John Peel when he's far, far away
With his hounds and his horn in the morning?

"Unnethe" can be heard by flexible ears as "uneasily," for indeed the drunken Miller sits insecurely, uneasily, upon his horse. But the rest of the passage—and *The Canterbury Tales* as a whole—we can read rapidly, understanding most of it, and missing of course many smaller points. But it is not a foreign language to us. We can at least read it fairly rapidly.

When we arrive at Edmund Spenser's *The Faerie Queene* (1590) we find the English (termed "early modern English") a bit easier. It was used for almost 200 years, from the beginning of the Tudor period (1485) until 1649. It ended, scholars say, with the interregnum (all that stuff with Cromwell and others, 1649-60) and the restoration of the Stuarts to the throne (with Charles II in 1660).

From Book I, Canto I, of *The Faerie Queene* we find:

A Gentle Knight was pricking on the plaine,
Y cladd in mightie armes and silver shielde,
Wherein old dints of deepe wounds did remaine,
The cruell markes of many a bloudy fielde;
Yet armes till that time did he never wield:
His angry steede did chide his foming bitt,
As much disdayning to the curbe to yield:
Full jolly knight he seemd, and faire did sitt,
As one for knightly giusts and fierce encounters fitt.

But on his brest a bloudie Crosse he bore,
The deare remembrance of his dying Lord,
For whose sweete sake that glorious badge he wore,
And dead as living ever him ador'd:
Upon his shield the like was also scor'd,
For soveraine hope, which in his helpe he had:

> *Right faithfull true he was in deede and word,*
> *But of his cheere did seeme too solemne sad;*
> *Yet nothing did he dread, but ever was ydrad.*

"Pricking" is strange to our ears; it means to urge forward with a sharp point or spur. The "Y" of line two is a preening archaism affected by Spenser simply to mean the past participle of "cladd," which is clothed. So, the knight was clothed with armor and a silver shield. "Chide" is known to us today as to scold or reproach, so the horse is pushing against, reproaching, his bit. "Giusts" we recognize as jousts. "Soveraine" we correctly feel must mean sovereign, hence superior (and in the meaning of the poem, "holy'). "Ydrad" is another willful preening archaism of Spenser, meaning simply the past participle of the verb dread. So the knight was always deemed formidable or dreaded.

Shakespeare writes from 1590 to 1613, in the late phase of early modern English We find him much easier than Spenser:

> *Seyton!—I am sick at heart,*
> *When I behold—Seyton, I say!—This push*
> *Will cheer me ever, or disseat me now.*
> *I have lived long enough: my way of life*
> *Is fall'n into the sear, the yellow leaf;*
> *And that which should accompany old age,*
> *As honour, love, obedience, troops of friends,*
> *I must not look to have; but, in their stead,*
> *Curses, not loud but deep, mouth-honour, breath,*
> *Which the poor heart would fain deny, and dare not.*
> *Macbeth, Act V, Scene 3*

Which brings us to Edgar Allan Poe's 1847 "Ulalume," which presents us with no language problems—

> *The skies they were ashen and sober;*

The leaves they were crispéd and sere—
The leaves they were withering and sere;
It was night in the lonesome October
Of my most immemorial year;
It was hard by the dim lake of Auber,
In the misty mid region of Weir—
It was down by the dank tarn of Auber,
In the ghoul-haunted woodland of Weir.

Which brings us to Billy Joel's 1973 "Piano Man:"

Now Paul is a real estate novelist
Who never had time for a wife
And he's talkin' with Davy, who's still in the Navy
And probably will be for life.
And the waitress is practicing politics
As the businessmen slowly get stoned,
Yes, they're sharing a drink they call loneliness
But it's better than drinkin' alone.

Columbia, 1973

Here a word person has more than just straightforward simple meaning.

A "real estate novelist" is not what the line seems to say, a novelist writing about real estate, but rather a full-time real estate salesman who is trying to write a novel. "Never had time for a wife" may be a simple statement of fact, but implies something about Paul's priorities: As is often the case with lyrics, the listener is free to speculate.

Davy's Navy career is not just a fact; it is looked at (perhaps) with disappointment by the singer, the piano man. "Practicing" has two meanings—(1) trying to speak about politics knowledgeably, and (2) really being a political person advancing herself with her customers.

"Stoned" is of course 1960s modern speak for intoxicated, never available to Chaucer, Spenser, Shakespeare, or Poe.

Possessing a foreign language

But what about a second language? So far, I have been speaking of a facile "word person" whose only language is English. But a person who has this facility for words, for hearing their overtones, for making connections, even distant connections, in the symphony of language, is preselected for heightened success and joy if he should be introduced to a second language.

Etymology becomes for such a person not just a strange English vocabulary word coming from Greek, but an adventure in the derivation of words. If your second language should be Latin or any Romance language, "conjugal" quickly deconstructs to Latin "*cum*" (with) and "*juga*" (yoke). Hence, yoked together, married.

"Fraternal," from Latin "*frater*" (brother). Hence, "brotherly." From there the leap to "sorority" is easy. "President" resolves to Latin "*pre*" (before) and "*sedere*" (to sit). Hence, he who sits up front. "Tangent" is recognized as coming from Latin "*tangere*," to touch.

Each brain is different

Let us remember, as an aside here, that there are people who can listen to music with lyrics—or even attend to dialog on TV—while accurately performing a complex second task. Math, for example, or writing a letter. And there are those—I am one—who cannot. We are one-task-at-a-time people. But some of those one-task-at-a-time people—and again I am one—can listen to wordless baroque music and study for the bar exam.

But there are some people who must have part of their brain distracted in order effectively to use the rest of their brain. Each of us is different; each of us is unique; each of us learns differently. This is important for teachers to remember.

John Locke remembered it, as he spoke of the individuality of every person, each with unalienable rights.

Some people are open to poetry, and some are not. The people who are not, well, they find poetry to be stilted, artificial, precious, and boring. But the facility for poetry need not accompany the facility for a second language, just facility for language in general. And the facility for poetry comes late to some. It came late to me.

If your second language is a Germanic one, you delight in the discovery that "dirigible" or "blimp" in German is *Luftschiff*—two words put together: *Luft* (air) and *Schiff* (ship). "Airship." And you are pleased that "helicopter" is *Hub* (lift) and *Schrauber* (screwer). "Lift screwer." Or, to go back to the Greek, *heli* and Latin *capere*, "twist grabber."

You will also be delighted that our English "kindergarten" is two German words, *Kinder* (children) and *Garten* (garden). And because you can see that "o'erhanging" is really two words, you quickly realize that German *"Kindergartenlehrerin"* must be three words, the Germans doing that odd thing of writing compound words as one long word.

Where did English come from?

Your road into a second language is much smoother if your second language is one which contributed to the development of English. Over 60% of all English words have Greek or Latin roots. So, if Greek is your second language (rare for Americans) or your second language is Latin or one of its children (the so-called Romance languages)—French, Spanish, Portuguese, Italian, Romanian—you have a massive head start. French and Latin alone participate in 58% of English words.

Words of Greek origin generally entered English in one of three ways:

- indirectly by way of Latin,

- borrowed directly from Greek writers, or
- especially in the case of scientific terms, formed in modern times by combining Greek elements in new ways. Only 6% of English words come directly from Greek.

You also have a great head start if your second language is Germanic (German, Dutch, Danish, Norwegian, Swedish, Yiddish, Afrikaans). 26% of English words come from the Germanic languages. There is a smidgen of Slavic in English but that smidgen could be erased and we would not notice the absence.

Nothing comes into English from Finnish or Hungarian, the so-called Finno-Ugric language family, because those languages were developed on Mars and came to earth in a capsule around 1970.

Cognates

John Keats said, "A thing of beauty is a joy for ever." So is a cognate, a "sound-alike.". You comprehend it immediately and you possess it forever. "Espada" in Spanish is "spade" in English, whether you are learning English as your second language, or you are an English speaker and Spanish is your second language. Spanish "motosierra" yields to you as "motor saw," because "motor," is an obvious cognate with "moto," and "serration" is a veiled cognate of serration. The Sierra Nevada mountains are the snowed-upon serration.

Word families

The vistas of word families opens to you if you have the facility to play with language. For example, the word "home" takes you to:

- *Homebody*
- *Homing pigeon*
- *Homesick*
- *Homely*

- *Stay-at-home*

Or the word "port" from the Latin for "carry" takes you to:

- *Portable*
- *Porter*
- *Portage*
- *Report*
- *Import*
- *Deport*
- *Disport*
- *Portmanteau*

This playing with words may remind you somewhat of the variations you learned when you began reading phonically:

- cake, bake, take, make, lake;
- cry, fry, spry, try, my, fly
- ball, hall, call, tall

Surprises

And last but not least, there are the joys of finding odd thoughts in a second language—thoughts we just don't have in English. Two of my favorites from German are *"Leinen faltet edel,"*—"Linen wrinkles nobly," and *"Den Teufel nicht auf die Wand malen,"*— "Don't paint the devil on the wall."

I suspect that the fastidiously neat Germans needed a fine-sounding rationale for appearing a bit rumpled in their linens. But as to the second one, meaning, "Don't borrow trouble by speaking of it," I can only suspect there might be something of the story of Faust spooking around. Who knows?

Afterword

Thank you for completing the journey. You have honored me by reading this small book. I know that some of it was difficult, particularly that last chapter.

I hope that my posited triad of politics, faith, and love has become fleshed out for you so much that it will be useful in your own life. That was my goal.

If I have been successful or somewhat so, I owe it to God. If I have failed you, the failure is my own.

Acknowledgements

—Jim Tipton, friend, companion, colleague, co-conspirator;

—Tucker Montgomery, Bill Snyder, Don Horton, and John Mack each of whom at various times saved my life;

—Assistant Rector of the Church of the Ascension, Christopher Hogin, son of my law partner, friend, spiritual guide, proofreader;

—Pat Bright, businesswoman, selfless public servant, colleague, rescuer of cats;

—Irina Bancos, Mayo Clinic endocrinologist, thinker, Romanian, friend;

—Claude Dalton, fellow shooter, political ally;

—Mary Beth Hood, tireless mother, amazing worker;

—My judicial law clerks who taught me so much through the years: Elisabeth Bellinger, Jimmy Carter, Sharon Eun, John Higgins, Ryann Musick Jeffers, Holly Martin, Tina Osborn, Patrick Rose, Luke Shipley, Stephanie Epperson Stuart, Megan Swain;

—Ted Bruning, who for four years, 1956-1960, pounded on the child who came to Webb School, until I could write and think competently;

—B.E. Sharp, Webb School's teacher of life skills on and off the football field;

—Robert Webb, who taught me the joys of Latin and made Ted Bruning and B.E. Sharp possible;

—Steve Bailey, Fred Brackney, Jack Brakebill, Randy Overbey,

Bobby Sherwood, and Doug White, who have guided and continue to guide my religious growth;

—Miss Freeman, my Tyson Junior High School seventh-grade English teacher, who taught me the structure of language;

—John Sobieski, the world's finest law professor;

—and Carl Pierce, who had the grace to admit Mary and me to law school.

Endnotes

ENDNOTE 1: FINAL ORDER

This is Judge Rosenbalm's final order, concluding *Rose v. Swann*. It incorporates by reference an orally-delivered memorandum opinion. That opinion is set out in ENDNOTE 2. This method of "incorporation by reference" is commonly done for simplicity and thoroughness. Everything a judge of a "court of record" says in concluding a case is transcribed by a court reporter and becomes part of the final order.

IN THE CIRCUIT COURT FOR KNOX COUNTY, TENNESSEE

WENDY WHITMAN ROSE

   Plaintiff

   vs.   **No. 3-464-06**

WILLIAM KIRK SWANN

   Defendant

ORDER

This cause came on to be heard on the 11th day of May, 2012, before the Honorable Wheeler A. Rosenbalm, Judge, holding the Circuit Court for Knox County, Tennessee, Division III, upon the renewed Motion for Summary Judgment filed on behalf of the Defendant together with the Affidavit, Memorandum and other supporting materials filed therewith in addition to the previously filed Motion for Summary Judgment on behalf of the Defendant and all supporting documents and materials filed therewith, the briefs and arguments in opposition on behalf of the Plaintiff, together with all briefs, affidavits, memoranda and other documents in opposition previously filed, the argument of counsel, and the record as a whole, from all of which it appeared that the Motion of the Defendant was well taken and should be granted. The Court announced its opinion from the bench, which opinion has been contemporaneously recorded and is appended hereto and made a part hereof by reference as fully and completely as if specifically and verbatim copied herein.

IT IS, THEREFORE, ORDERED that the Motion for Summary Judgment of the Defendant be and the same is hereby granted and that this cause of action shall, in all respects, be and the same is hereby dismissed.

IT IS FURTHER ORDERED that the opinion of the Court announced from the bench on the 11th day of May, 2012, a verbatim copy of which is appended hereto, shall be made a part of this Order by reference as fully and completely as if specifically set forth verbatim herein.

IT IS FURTHER ORDERED that the costs of the Court be assessed against the Plaintiff and her Surety for which execution may be awarded.

ENTER this 21st day of May, 2012.

_____

Hon. Wheeler Rosenbalm, Judge

APPROVED:

_____

Richard L. Hollow
Attorney for Defendant

CERTIFICATE OF SERVICE

I certify that a true and exact copy of the foregoing Order has been served upon the following counsel of record by placing same in the United States Mail, postage prepaid, this _____ day of May, 2012:

Russell L. Egli
Attorney at Law
11470 Parkside Drive, Suite 201
Knoxville, TN 37934

John E. Herbison Attorney at Law
1310 Madison Street
Clarksville, TN 37040

This certification is provided in accordance with Rule 58 of the Tennessee Rules of Civil Procedure.

s/ Richard L. Hollow

ENDNOTE 2: MEMORANDUM
OPINION, MAY 11, 2012

THE COURT: Okay. Thank you very much. I thank both of you. I appreciate your arguments. This case has been of great interest to me for a long time. It has been pending a long time. It was filed back in 2006, shortly after the election that is part of the subject matter of this lawsuit. It's been of peculiar interest to me because I have always been intrigued by some of the legal principles and problems in our society that bring various legal prooositions or principles in conflict with one another.

The rights that we give parties to bring suits for defamation often collide with the rights that are given to our citizens under the First Amendment, and that collision and competition of ideas has always been of great interest to me.

I have always been somewhat intrigued by defamation lawsuits also because one of my heroes in the legal world was Louis Nizer. As you all probably remember, in his day, Louis Nizer was a leading advocate in the field of defamation, libel, and slander, and his book, *My Life in Court*, has always been sort of an inspiration to me and, of course, this is an important case because it involves questions about the breadth of the First Amendment rights and the role of First Amendment in the role of public debate in our public affairs.

So the case has been intriguing to me from the outset, and I have devoted a lot of time thinking about this case. Of course, we've been here now on two Motions for Summary Judgment, and I have read and studied most all of the authorities that you all have cited. Of course, many of those authorities I have studied and relied upon both as a practitioner and in other defamation lawsuits here in this court.

Of course, we did have a previous hearing on a Motion for Summary Judgment, which I would consider to be limited or partial in nature. That Motion did not, as I interpreted it, set forth with any great specificity any reliance upon the argument that the language employed by Judge Swann in this instance was not defamatory. That was wrapped up, of course, or addressed in the arguments that Mr. Hollow made in the brief that he filed, and we talked about that some on the last occasion.

I denied the last motion. I think it's important to note I denied that first motion for Summary Judgment largely because of my concern about whether it could pass muster under the standards that have been established *Hannan v. Alltel Publishing Company*. In that first motion, the defendant principally argued that there was insufficient evidence here to show that any statements by Judge Swann were uttered with actual malice under the United States Supreme Court decisions that addressed those First Amendment considerations, and relying upon *Hannan*, and more specifically, I believe, *Blair v. West Town Mall*, it was my impression that Judge Swann had not negated in the fashion required by *Hannan*, had not negated the issue of actual malice, but this Motion today is different.

It addresses the question more specifically whether the language used by Judge Swann can be considered defamatory in nature, and it certainly addresses the question of whether the issue about actual malice has been negated, because Judge Swann has now filed a very comprehensive affidavit that, in my judgment, clearly negates the issue of actual malice.

So I think we have a different situation here today. When it comes to this Court's authority to revisit this issue, I would point out that the denial of the first Motion for Summary Judgment was clearly not a Final Order, and in my opinion, very humble opinion, this Court can review a non Final Order at any time under any circumstances that the Court feels appropriate, but I think more importantly, Rule 66, with which we deal here, I think points out that these Motions can be filed at any time, and in my judgment, that means they can be revisited if they have been denied.

Rule 56.02 says, "A party against whom a claim and so forth

is asserted may, at any time, move, with or without supporting affidavits, for a summary judgment in the party's favor as to all or any part thereof." So I feel quite comfortable in reviewing and revisiting what has been done on a former occasion.

It is abundantly clear in this case that there is one matter about which I don't believe anyone could argue or regard as disputed, and that is the fact that the plaintiff, Wendy Whitman Rose, for the purposes of this proceeding, was a public figure. She, for her own purposes and to serve her own personal interest, became engaged and embroiled in a very contentious political contest.

As I understand the record, she agreed to support Judge Swann's opponent, Mr. Lee, because she thought, according to her explanation, that would secure for her some relief from Judge Swann's supervision over her divorce litigation, She, as the evidence shows quite clearly, played a very active and important role in Mr. Lee's campaign against Judge Swann. So it is clear, at least to this Court—and I think it's undisputed—that Mrs. Rose was, at the time of these events, a public figure, and by becoming a public figure, she became bound by the provisions of the First Amendment that provide, according to the rulings of the United States Supreme Court, that statements made by others about her conduct and participation in this election would not be actionable, even if they were false, unless she could show that those statements were made with actual malice, that is, they they were made with knowledge of their falsity or with reckless disregard as to whether they were true or false.

So the burden is upon her in this instance before she can proceed with this case to show that Judge was guilty of actual malice or employed actual malice in the statements that he made. Judge Swann has shifted the burden to Mrs. Rose to go forward with that evidence, if any she has, by the filing of the comprehensive and exhaustive affidavit that he has filed in this case, which negates, in the opinion of this Court, any actual malice.

So after reviewing this record with great care, I'm constrained to conclude that there is no showing of actual malice on the part of Judge Swann, that the plaintiff has not come forward with that kind of evidence. Her very able counsel argues that the words that were employed here could suggest that to some person, but this Court must most respectfully beg to differ.

It's clear here and undisputed in this case what the statements by Judge Swann are which are relied upon by the plaintiff in support of her claim of defamation. It's already been alluded to here in argument, but perhaps I should re-summarize the fact that Judge Swann is said to have made three statements here about which the plaintiff complains.

He told a reporter for the News-Sentinel that statements to the effect that he was impatient with some litigants was ludicrous. He commented during a discussion on a TV program called Inside Tennessee that the campaign by Mr. Lee and the manner in which it was conducted was, in his opinion, sleazy. His campaign committee adopted an advertisement put together by a number of supporting lawyers, lawyers who supported Judge Swann in this community, in which the campaign ad said, among other things, that the lawyers did not want the people going to the polls and selecting a Fourth Circuit judge based upon half truths.

Somehow, Mrs Rose perceives that that is tantamount to calling her a liar, a conclusion and argument with which also this Court would disagree and beg to differ, but this Court cannot find that there's anything in these statements or the evidence in the record to indicate that these comments were directed towards Mrs. Rose, and frankly, the Court is constrained to wonder whether anybody would know if they had anything to do with her activities in this campaign unless, perhaps, she told them, but I don't know that. That's a comment, an interjection, but I do not believe that these comments that are attributed to Judge Swann are capable of conveying a defamatory meaning to a reasonable person under the circumstances that we have to consider applicable to this case.

They are, and I agree with the defendant about this, they are the kind of language employed in political campaigns. Whether that's good or bad is not the issue for us to decide today, because when it comes to matters of public affairs and public figures are involved, our United States Supreme Court has decided, I think, with good reason, to say that we have to open up the valve of communication and comment and debate, and under these circumstances, we have to recognize that this is the kind of language that frequently occurs in political campaigns, and perhaps on some occasions it's necessary to get people's attention, and certainly we should try to gather the voters' attention in all of these political affairs.

So it is the opinion of this Court, based upon the many, many, authorities from Tennessee jurisprudence that have discussed this issue, that these statements attributed to Judge Swann by the plaintiff in the case are rhetorical, political hyperbole that do not rise to the level of defamation, certainly not defamation of Mrs. Rose in this instance.

It appears to the Court that the plaintiff's claim for intentional infliction of emotional distress or outrageous conduct must rise or fall on the question of whether or not the plaintiff has an actionable case of defamation, but notwithstanding that, if the allegations in the Complaint are examined with care, consistent with the Tennessee decisions that define the relatively new tort of outrageous conduct and intentional infliction of emotional distress, it appears to the Court that that examination reveals that this is not the kind of egregious conduct which would compel people in the community that hear about it to exclaim "Outrageous!"

As a matter of fact, it would appear to the Court that if people of the community were fully informed about the context in which the words attributed to Judge Swann were uttered, that instead of exclaiming "Outrageous," they would be prone to say, "Well, that's the way it is in politics." "If you can't stand the heat, you stay out of the kitchen."

So I can most respectfully—and not intending any disrespect

by that kind of commentary—I most respectfully must conclude that the Complaint simply fails to state a claim upon which relief can be granted for intentional infliction of emotional distress.

I find the plaintiff's argument about the applicability of Section 1983 of the—I can't even remember the title of it now—the United States Code.

MR. HOLLOW: 42.

THE COURT: 42. Thank you.

MR. HOLLOW: John you should have been quicker on that one.

THE COURT: I find the plaintiff's argument about the applicability of the Title 42, Section 1983 of the United States Code or what's commonly referred to as civil rights cases, to be very interesting, but it appears to the Court that, in this case, it is without dispute that Judge Swann was not acting under color of law when these circumstances that form the basis of this case occurred.

As a matter of fact, Judge Swann was not acting in any judicial capacity or as a representative of the state during this political campaign. The political process simply reduced Judge Swann to nothing more than a political candidate. He was not acting as a judicial officer. So in my opinion, the inclusion of the civil rights section or theory in this Complaint does not help or enhance the plaintiff's lawsuit, and it is the opinion of the Court that, in this case, an action based upon 42 U.S.C. §1983 has not been stated or established.

So most respectfully, the Court is constrained to conclude, after much discussion with you gentlemen on these two occasions, which the Court appreciates, and with the considerable study of the record in this case and the authorities that pertain to this case, that the Motion for Summary Judgement filed by the defendant in this lawsuit is well taken, and it is respectfully granted.

Mr. Hollow, if you will please prepare an appropriate Order, we'll get that entered. Thank you for being back with us, Mr.

Herbison, and we look forward to seeing you both again. You may adjourn Court until 9:00 Monday morning.

END OF PROCEEDINGS

ENDNOTE 3: ACT OUT OF DUTY

I learned in 2016 that doing the right thing out of duty and not for some ulterior motive is exactly what Immanuel Kant describes and praises as the only basis of moral action. Kant lays this out in his 1785 *Groundwork of the Metaphysics of Morals* (*Grundlegung zur Metaphysik der Sitten*). The fact that it took me until 2016 to learn about Kant's description of duty demonstrates not only my slow learning curve but also Kant's brilliance more than two hundred years ago.

ENDNOTE FOUR: JOHN LOCKE

However, John Locke (1632-1704) did not believe that self-ownership included the right to commit suicide. In this and certain other ways he varies from "pure" libertarianism.

Locke's *Second Treatise of Government* (1689) states in section 6:

> ... *The state of nature has a law of nature to govern it, which obliges every one: and reason, which is that law, teaches all mankind, who will but consult it, that being all equal and independent, no one ought to harm another in his life, health, liberty, or possessions: for men being all the workmanship of one omnipotent, and infinitely wise maker; all*

the servants of one sovereign master, sent into the world by his order, and about his business; they are his property, whose workmanship they are, made to last during his, not one another's pleasure: and being furnished with like faculties, sharing all in one community of nature, there cannot be supposed any such subordination among us, that may authorize us to destroy one another, as if we were made for one another's uses, as the inferior ranks of creatures are for our's. Every one, as he is bound to preserve himself, and not to quit his station wilfully, so by the like reason, when his own preservation comes not in competition, ought he, as much as he can, to preserve the rest of mankind, and may not, unless it be to do justice on an offender, take away, or impair the life, or what tends to the preservation of the life, the liberty, health, limb, or goods of another.
(Emphasis mine)

However, Locke makes it clear in sections 7, 8, and 11 that one can use restraint, and even violence, against another to preserve the common good:

Sect. 7. And that all men may be restrained from invading others rights, and from doing hurt to one another, and the law of nature be observed, which willeth the peace and preservation of all mankind, the execution of the law of nature is, in that state, put into every man's hands, whereby everyone has a right to punish the transgressors of that law to such a degree, as may hinder its violation: for the law of nature would, as all other laws that concern men in this world be in vain, if there were no body that in the state of nature had a power to execute that law, and thereby preserve the innocent and restrain offenders. And if anyone in the state of nature may punish another for any evil he has done, every one may do so: for in that state of perfect equality, where naturally there is no superiority or jurisdiction of one over another, what any may do in prosecution of that law, everyone must needs have a right to do.

Sect. 8. And thus, in the state of nature, one man comes by a power over another; but yet no absolute or arbitrary power, to use a criminal, when he has got him in his hands, according to the passionate heats, or boundless extravagancy of his own will; but only to retribute to him, so far as calm reason and conscience dictate, what is proportionate to his transgression, which is so much as may serve for reparation and restraint: for these two are the only reasons, why one man may lawfully do harm to another, which is that we call punishment. In transgressing the law of nature, the offender declares himself to live by another rule than that of reason and common equity, which is that measure God has set to the actions of men, for their mutual security; and so he becomes dangerous to mankind, the tye, which is to secure them from injury and violence, being slighted and broken by him. Which being a trespass against the whole species, and the peace and safety of it, provided for by the law of nature, every man upon this score, by the right he hath to preserve mankind in general, may restrain, or where it is necessary, destroy things noxious to them, and so may bring such evil on anyone, who hath transgressed that law, as may make him repent the doing of it, and thereby deter *him, and by his example others, from doing the like mischief. And in the case, and upon this ground, EVERY MAN HATH A RIGHT TO PUNISH THE OFFENDER, AND BE EXECUTIONER OF THE LAW OF NATURE.*

Sect. 11. . . . and thus it is, that every man, in the state of nature, has a power to kill a murderer, both to deter others from doing the like injury, which no reparation can compensate, by the example of the punishment that attends it from everybody, and also to secure men from the attempts of a criminal, who having renounced reason, the common rule and measure God hath given to mankind, hath, by the unjust violence and slaughter he hath committed upon one, declared war against all mankind, and therefore may be destroyed as a lion or a tyger, one of those wild savage beasts, with whom men can have no society nor security: and upon this is grounded that great law of nature, Whoso sheddeth man's blood, by man shall his blood be shed.

ENDNOTE FIVE: LIBERTARIANISM

A libertarian in most ways, Locke in sections 138, 139, and 140 of his *Second Treatise* sets up a regimen for consent to taxation:

Sect. 138. . . . the supreme power [the legislature] cannot take from any man any part of his property without his own consent: for <u>the preservation of property being the end of government, and that for which men enter into society,</u> it necessarily *supposes and requires, that the people should have property, without which they must be supposed to lose that, by entering into society, which was the end for which they entered into it; too gross an absurdity for any man to own. Men therefore in society having property, they have such a right to the goods, which by the law of the community are their's, that no body hath a right to take their substance or any part of it from them, without their own consent: without this they have no property at all; <u>for I have truly no property in that, which another can by right take from me, when he pleases, against my consent.</u> Hence it is a mistake to think, that the supreme or legislative power of any commonwealth, can do what it will, and dispose of the estates of the subject arbitrarily, or take any part of them at pleasure. This is not much to be feared in governments where the legislative consists, wholly or in part, in assemblies which are variable, whose members, upon the dissolution of the assembly, are subjects under the common laws of their country, equally with the rest . . .* (Emphasis mine.)

Sect. 139. But government, into whatsoever hands it is put, being, as I have before shewed, intrusted with this condition, and for this end, that men might have and secure their properties; the prince, or senate, however it may have power to make laws, for the regulating of property between the subjects one amongst another, yet can never have a power to take to themselves the whole, or any part of the subjects property, without their own consent: for this would be in effect to leave them no property at all . . .

Sect. 140. It is true, governments cannot be supported without great charge, and it is fit every one who enjoys his share of the protection, should pay out of his estate his proportion for the maintenance of it. But still it must be with his own consent, i.e. the consent of the majority, giving it either by themselves, or their representatives chosen by them: for if any one shall claim a power to lay and levy taxes on the people, by his own authority, and without such consent of the people, he thereby invades the fundamental law of property, and subverts the end of government: for what property have I in that, which another may by right take, when he pleases, to himself? (Emphasis mine)

ENDNOTE SIX: DOWN EAST

In a Marshall Dodge and Bob Bryan skit, "Which Way to Millinocket?," (*Bert and I... And Other Stories from Down East,* 1958) there is the now-famous line, "You can't get there from here."

ENDNOTE 7: OBITUARY, JEANETTE MAE (YOUNG) SWANN, 7 SEPTEMBER 1914-18 NOVEMBER 2005

(Knoxville News Sentinel, 19 November 2005)

Jeanette Young Swann was born in Hancock, Maine (pop. 600), in 1914. She walked to school and carried her lunch. Whenever possible, she traded her own lunch (chicken sandwiches) for Gladys Colwell's lobster sandwiches. Gladys was tired of lobster, as her parents owned Colwell's lobster pound. Jeanette never, ever, got tired of lobster.

She wanted to be a nurse. Because she couldn't get enough science courses in Hancock to be accepted to nursing school, she spent a post-high school year at Maine Central Institute in Pittsfield. At age eighteen, after MCI, she borrowed the tuition for nursing school, and boarded a bus for Boston.

She trained at the Peter Bent Brigham Hospital, receiving her R.N., and rose to be head nurse in pediatrics at that hospital. From there she became head nurse at the Harvard College Infirmary in Cambridge, Massachusetts.

Along the way she met a handsome, penniless medical student who—after a whirlwind courtship—"married her for her money" ($100/month). When they spent some of it extravagantly, it would be at the Copley Plaza, for lobster Newburg.

When she and William K. Swann Jr., MD, came to Knoxville in 1949, Jeanette helped build his fledgling thoracic practice by entertaining referring doctors with "shore dinners." This was not easy. The lobsters had to come by train in wooden barrels from Damariscotta, Maine. On top of seaweed and ice. Some made it, some didn't. The ones alive got boiled. The dead ones got thermidored. No one got ptomaine, and the medical practice grew.

Jeanette was an energetic homemaker and gardener. She was a longtime member of the Knoxville Academy of Medicine Alliance. She was a mainstay supporter of the Knoxville Opera Company, and active as well with Ossoli and the Knoxville Symphony. It is particularly fitting that her home of forty years was the Show House of the Knoxville Symphony Society in 2005.

She is survived by three sons, six grandchildren, two great-grandchildren, and wonderful caregivers and friends at the Homewood Residence at Deane Hill. The family particularly *appreciates the years of loving care provided by our friend, and Jeanette's friend, Ms. June Lamb.*

The body is at the Mann's Heritage Chapel in Bearden, where the family will receive friends from 4 to 6 pm on Monday, 21 November. Burial will be private. In lieu of flowers, please consider a memorial to the Community Coalition on Family Violence (1301 Hannah Avenue, Knoxville, TN 37921), or the Knoxville Opera Company.

ENDNOTE 8: CHRONOLOGY

- 17 January 1913: Birth of my father, William Kirk Swann Jr., at Between, Georgia
- 7 September 1914: birth of my mother, Jeanette Mae Young (Swann) at Hancock, Maine
- 23 June 1938: My father graduates from Harvard Medical School
- 7 December 1941: Pearl Harbor is bombed. My father enlists in Army.
- 1 August 1942: The 22d Field Hospital is activated at Camp White, Oregon, under command of my father, 1st Lt. William K. Swann Jr. The original cadre was of 22 men, including my father, all of whom had come from Bradley Field, Windsor Locks, Connecticut.
- 30 September 1942: I am born in Boston, Massachusetts
- 20 November 1942: Lt. Col. Willis D Butler assumes command of the 22d Field Hospital, relieving my father.
- 1947-49: I attend kindergarten and first grade at the George H. Conley Elementary School in Hyde Park, Massachusetts, a suburb of Boston.
- 1949-52: I attend second through fourth grades at Van Gilder School (now razed) at the corner of 13th and

Highland, Knoxville, Tennessee. I live at 1920 West Clinch Avenue in the Fort Sanders neighborhood. 1920 West Clinch was a duplex. The side yard and backyard gave onto an alley which ran parallel to and between Clinch and White Avenue. Across the alley lived my best friend, Brent Soper. After many years the duplex was razed and replaced by the Thompson Cancer Survival Center.

- 1952-54: I attend fifth and sixth grades at Sequoyah Elementary School in the Sequoyah Hills neighborhood.
- 30 September 1953: I turn eleven, old enough for Boy Scouts, and join Troop Five at St. John's Episcopal church, Knoxville, Tennessee.
- Summer 1954: age eleven, Boy Scout Camp Pellissippi on Norris Lake, Anderson County, Tennessee. I learn to shoot, using a bolt-action, single-shot .22 rifle, and win the camp championship. My teacher was an Iranian military officer.
- 1954-56: I attend Tyson Junior High School for the seventh and eighth grades.
- Summer 1955: age twelve, Camp Pellissippi.
- Summer 1956: age thirteen, Camp Pellissippi. Order of the Arrow Ordeal.
- 1956-60: I attend the Webb School of Knoxville for grades nine through twelve.
- Fall 1956: I become Senior Patrol Leader for Troop Five.
- Summer 1957, age fourteen, Camp Pellissippi.
- 12-18 July 1957: National Boy Scout Jamboree, Valley Forge, Pennsylvania; attendance 52,580.
- 15 February 1961: My father puts a pacemaker into 26-year-old Mary Gentry's chest. She then was the world's youngest pacemaker recipient.
- 1960-64: Harvard College
- Summer 1961: I work atop Mt. Leconte
- 13 August 1961: Berlin wall is begun

- 1964-65: Fulbright Fellowship, Graz, Austria
- July 1965: Summer language school in Santander, Spain, on the Bay of Biscay, Universidad Menendez Pelayo. I meet Mary Kathleen Cunningham
- 17 September 1966: Mary and I marry in Rochester, New York
- 1965-68: Yale University, first three years of graduate school
- 1968-69: Yale Berlin Fellowship, Freie Universität, West Berlin
- 1969-70: Yale University, final year of graduate school
- 1970-72: Brown University, Assistant Professor
- 1971: Yale University, Ph.D.
- 1972-75: University of Tennessee Law School
- 1974-75: Law clerk to Honorable James Parrott, Tennessee Court of Appeals, Eastern Grand Division, Knoxville
- 1975-79: Private practice, Kramer Rayson law firm
- 1979-82: Private practice, Hogin, Guyton, Swann & London law firm
- 1982-2014: Circuit Court judge, Sixth Judicial District of Tennessee
- 9 November 1989: Berlin wall falls
- 8 October 1990: death of William Kirk Swann Jr., MD, in Knoxville, Tennessee
- 17 November 1997: Diana and I marry, Chief Justice E. Riley Anderson officiating, in the courtroom of the Tennessee Supreme Court
- 18 November 2005: death of Jeanette May Young Swann, in Knoxville, Tennessee
- 8 September 2006: complaint filed in *Rose v. Swann*
- Spring 2012: Mary Gentry becomes the world's oldest living pacemaker recipient. (She had several replacements after her first implant done by my father.)

- 11 May 2012: memorandum opinion of Circuit Judge Wheeler Rosenbalm in *Rose v. Swann*
- 22 June 2012: end of six years of litigation in *Rose v. Swann*
- 29 October 2014: surgery to repair dissecting aneurysm of my ascending aorta
- 2016: *Five Proofs of Christianity* published (WestBow Press)

ENDNOTE 9: TIME

Daylight savings time began in World War One, and was supposed to be a temporary wartime expedient, but is now, it seems, permanent law pursuant to the Uniform Time Act of 1966, Pub. L. 89-387, 80 Stat. 107, signed by President Lyndon B. Johnson 13 April 1966. As I said elsewhere, whether good or bad, government programs never die. They expand.

ENDNOTE 10: U-6 VERSUS U-3
THE BUREAU OF LABOR STATISTICS

The Bureau's U-6 number is defined as "total unemployed, plus all persons marginally attached to the labor force, plus total employed part time for economic reasons, as a percent of the civilian labor force plus all persons marginally attached to the labor force."

In a note the Bureau explains that "persons marginally attached to the labor force are those who currently are neither working nor looking for work but indicate that they want and are available for a job and have looked for work sometime in the past 12 months. Discouraged workers, a subset of the marginally attached, have given a job-market related reason for not currently looking for work. <u>Persons employed part time for economic reasons</u> are those who want and are available for full-time work but have had to settle for a part-time schedule." (Emphasis mine.)

Because of Obamacare, part time employment is preferred by employers to avoid Obamacare-mandated insurance coverage.

The U-3 number, on the other hand, is defined as "total unemployed, as a percent of the civilian labor force (official unemployment rate)." When an administration, or its media, deem U-3 the "official" rate, it is simply seeking to make that administration look better.

ENDNOTE 11

In letter 14 of C.S. Lewis's 1942 *Screwtape Letters,* senior demon Screwtape instructs his nephew, the incompetent junior tempter Wormwood, that God (called by Screwtape and all the demons "the Enemy") really loves humans: "For we must never forget what is the most repellent and inexplicable trait in our Enemy; He really loves the hairless bipeds He has created and always gives back to them with His right hand what He has taken away with His left."

ENDNOTE 12

In Bob Dannals's "E-devotions: Inbox Inspirations," 22 February 2017.

ENDNOTE 13

Robert Nozick, "Distributive Justice," *Anarchy, State, and Utopia*. Basic Books, 1974.

ENDNOTE 14

Milton and Rose Friedman, "Created Equal," *Free to Choose, A Personal Statement*. Harcourt Brace & Co., 1980.

Printed in the United States
By Bookmasters